Teaching the Jesus Way

Building a Transformational Teaching Ministry

JAY JOHNSTON • RONALD K. BROWN
Introduction by BRUCE H. WILKINSON

ISBN 0-6330-0840-0

This book is a resource in the Leadership and Skill Development category of the Christian Growth Study Plan for course numbers LS-0049, LS-0053, and LS-0106.

Dewey Decimal Classification: 264.8
Subject Headings: CHRISTIAN EDUCATION
BIBLE—STUDY AND TEACHING
JESUS CHRIST—TEACHING METHODS

Printed in the United States of America

Sunday School Group
LifeWay Church Resources
127 Ninth Avenue, North
Nashville, Tennessee 37234

Cover design: Dale Royalty
Cover photography: Thom Hook

Acknowledgements:
Unless otherwise designated, all Scripture quotations are from **THE MESSAGE.** Copyright © 1993, 1995, 1996. Used by permission of NavPres Publishing Group.

Scripture quotations marked NIV are from the *Holy Bible New International Version.* Copyright ©1973, 1978, 1984 by International Bible Society.

Scripture quotations marked NASB are from the *New American Standard Bible.* © The Lockman Foundation, 1960, 1962, 1963, 1971, 1975, 1977. Used by permission.

Scripture quotations marked KJV are from *Holy Bible, King James Version.*

Contents

Foreword

Captioned beneath the photograph of a family gathered together is this probing question: "Is their Bible study changing the way they relate to each other?" It's a question every Sunday School leader needs to ask— and answer. How many believers think and live is not significantly different from nonbelievers.

To effect change we must teach for spiritual transformation. Spiritual transformation is God's work of changing a believer into the likeness of Jesus by creating a new identity in Christ and by empowering a lifelong relationship of love, trust, and obedience to glorify God.

In traveling across America, I have met many people whose lives have been transformed through an encounter with God's Word:

• An executive willing to unload a truckload of pipe so his Sunday School teacher could share the gospel with a truck owner;

• A mother in Boston who voluntarily served several churches in the New England area because she was so moved by needs;

• A teacher in Texas who left the comfort of her own growing church to teach the Bible in a struggling inter-city mission.

They heard a Bible lesson, but didn't stop there. They continued to interact with God's Truth, allowing it to change their lives.

This book is a resource in the *Teaching for Spiritual Transformation* series, designed to develop a Sunday School ministry focused on teaching for spiritual transformation. Each book helps leaders of a specific target group: general leaders, adults including young adults, youth, children, or preschoolers.

Teaching for spiritual transformation will yield thousands of believers who will give their best service to Christ. Then when we are confronted with questions like the one above, we can reply: "Yes. Bible study is changing the way they relate to each other, for the Christ they encounter in Scripture is changing their lives."

BILL L. TAYLOR,
DIRECTOR, SUNDAY SCHOOL GROUP

Introduction

A group of four- and five-year-olds had gathered for their Bible story time at church. One of the teachers asked, "Can someone tell us who is the special person God sent to show us how much He loves us?" A little girl eagerly waved her hand in the air and shouted, "I know! It's Mr. Dodd!"

What a wonderful mistake! Mr. Dodd, another teacher in the department, had made such an impression on this child that his name could be given as the answer to the teacher's question. This is teaching the Jesus way.

Could someone in your church say of his or her Bible study leader, "He teaches the way Jesus taught" or "She teaches just like Jesus"? If you are a teacher, have you ever said to yourself as you were preparing to lead a Bible study session, *I'm going to teach the Jesus way?*

We may prepare to teach with the needs of our learners in mind. We may study to develop an interesting lesson plan. But we sometimes forget to invest ourselves in an ongoing relationship with Jesus Christ, our model for teaching. We must learn of the Teacher before we can teach His way.

What happened when Jesus encountered people? He met the person; He interacted; and He taught, bringing the individual to a "stop sign" of personal decision and action. Those of us who are His followers are called to follow in His footsteps. Jesus not only wants us to *be* like Him, He also wants us to *teach* like Him.

Jesus' teaching ministry was one of spiritual transformation. When people came to know Jesus Christ and listened to what He said, they all were changed in some way. How many of your learners are really transformed? This book, and the entire *Teaching for Spiritual Transformation* series, is about helping build a transformational teaching ministry. As you study this material, you will be guided to think about how Jesus taught and how you can lead your teachers to be and to teach more like Him.

First, we need to assume His *mind-set.* There was no confusion in Jesus' mind regarding who He was or who His Father was. Jesus lived the way He did based on His relationship with His Heavenly Father. How would you answer if asked, Who are you? You might say you're someone's husband or wife, or that you live in a particular location, or that you do a particular job. All of those responses would be true. When a person receives Jesus Christ as Savior and Lord, however, he enters a new relationship with the Heavenly Father, a relationship that supercedes all others. Do you think more like the son or daughter of your physical parents or more like the son or daughter of your spiritual Father?

I challenge you to think, *I'm a son/daughter of God and I'm going to embrace God's agenda if I'm going to teach the way God wants me to teach.* Make a commitment to picture how Jesus would teach because you want to teach the Jesus way.

Why are you here? If you have accepted Christ as your personal Savior, your place is not on earth, it is in heaven. When you and God meet face-to-face in heaven, will not God's dream of spending time with you also come true? Then why are you still here? There must be a reason, a purpose in God's thinking. He has a mission for His teachers; something He wants to accomplish in and through their lives while they are in this world.

Mission—that's another principle for teaching the Jesus way. Leaders who have no purpose for their teaching or daily activities may teach with flair and be fascinated with the content, but they will not reach the goal God has for their lives. When Jesus was thinking about the cross, He knew that it was for this purpose that He came into the world. Jesus knew His purpose.

Have you discovered God's purpose for your life and ministry? Are you clearly focused on that mission? Are you doing something that will last, something that heaven will cheer; or are you doing something that only cheers your heart? If you are to teach the Jesus way, you will have that mission and purpose so clearly in mind that you go directly to it. Jesus took His Father's will and made it His own. Is that what you are doing? If not, then stop right now and pray, asking your Heavenly Father to let His will be done in your life.

Wouldn't it be something if the one Person in all of time who knew precisely His purpose and mission came directly to each teacher to give that teacher a mission? Wouldn't it be something if He took His mission and shared it with you? His mission would become your "co"-mission. Jesus already has done this by giving His disciples the Great Commission: "God authorized and commanded me to commission you: Go out and train everyone you meet, far and near, in this way of life, marking them by baptism in the threefold name: of the Father, Son, and Holy Spirit. Then instruct them in the practice of all I have commanded you. I'll be with you as you do this, day after day after day, right up to the end of the age" (Matt. 28:18b-20). Clearly, the Lord intends for those who teach His way to fulfill the Great Commission.

If a teacher is serious about being able to look back on his life to say, "What a fulfilling, significant, eternally-important life I lived! What a legacy I leave behind!," it will be because God's mission had become his. You and I can cooperate with God and one another in His mission, taking everything in our lives and focusing it all on that mission, not just in our teaching but in every aspect of our lives. To be a teacher, to teach for spiritual transformation is a high calling, one well worth "pressing on toward," as the Apostle Paul might say. Take the Master's mission and make it yours.

Teaching the Jesus way requires that we bear His *message*. In John 8:28 (NIV) Jesus said, "I do nothing on my own but speak just what the Father has taught me." What did Jesus do? He taught the Word of God.

Twenty-five years ago, I learned a valuable lesson. I was a young man preaching in a big church. I had prepared all week; I had developed a wonderful message with engrossing stories; I preached my heart out. When I had finished, I was satisfied that the message was well received by the congregation. After I had spoken and the congregation was exiting the building, I noticed an older woman standing off to the side. She came over and kindly said, "You know, I really enjoyed your thoughts, young man." As I was thanking her, though, she continued, "But I didn't come to hear your thoughts; I came to hear God's Word. Why on earth didn't you teach it?" Without another word, she turned and walked away.

Imagine the boldness that accompanied Moses as he came down from Mt. Sinai, carrying the tablets on which God had written His laws. When God's people on His mission engage others in the study of His message, there is no cause for timidity. Teachers have the oracles of God with the

Truth for everyone (1 Pet. 4:11, KJV).

Caution: A leader who attempts to teach God's Word with a sense of authority and boldness, but whose life stands in contradiction to God's Word is a barrier to spiritual transformation. That person is not a teacher of God's Truth, but rather an information-giver. Teachers who want God's message to connect with the lives of learners can enhance the environment for the work of the Holy Spirit if they will give attention to being an authentic witness of Christ in their daily living. You can set the example for teachers in your church through your own walk with God and your commitment to be a man or woman of God.

So many times we compartmentalize our teaching to a particular time and place. We think about coming away from our "normal life." When we enter a classroom, we assign our identity as a teacher to that setting. We identify the people who are in that room as the people we are responsible for teaching. Teaching the Jesus way changes that thinking. Whether the setting is a classroom, coffee break at work, lunch with someone in the neighborhood, or a game of tennis or golf, teaching can and does occur. God is not limited. Teachable people with teachable moments are precious to Him.

If you intend to build a teaching ministry based on the example of Jesus Christ, you will note that Jesus never stopped teaching. His school—His *marketplace* of learning—knew no boundaries. No matter who came to Him, Jesus started where people were and then ministered to them.

I am convinced that if you could draw a line around every moment of every day and every place Jesus went and were to ask Him "Where is your classroom?," He probably would smile and say, "Everywhere is my classroom. I want every person to learn of Me and be blessed."

Who are the people for whom you are responsible as a teacher? Some might say, "I am responsible for myself," and that is correct; we are responsible to God to give attention to the personal discipline of study as His child. Some might say, "I am responsible for teaching my family,"and that also is correct. Still, many Christian parents do not talk about God with their children nor do they teach their children about the Bible. Often this is because parents are uncomfortable with their own understanding of the Bible and/or lack ideas for teaching their children spiritual truth.

Churches with ministries that teach the Jesus way work to help parents with their roles as primary Bible teachers of their children.

For some, the marketplace extends to close friends. When a circumstance opens up, they may share the Bible with a friend, genuinely desiring God to work in that friend's life. Many will share about their faith, seek to influence their friends to follow Christ, and minister in a variety of ways. However, only a small percentage of the people who know Jesus Christ, who are on this mission and have this message, ever really go into the marketplace as Jesus did. It is difficult—even exhausting—for even the most dedicated teacher to look upon a marketplace with no boundaries. I wonder if I were to observe Jesus' teaching in my marketplace for a day, how often would I be shocked by the opportunities I had missed to join Him in teaching for transformation? I challenge you to think for a few moments about some ways you can teach for transformation in *your* marketplace.

Jesus taught differently every time. He changed His *method* depending on the person to whom He was relating. If question-answer was not working, He would start telling a story until He connected. Do you realize that, if you want to teach the Jesus way, you have absolute freedom and flexibility—and that you rarely would stand behind a desk or lectern and talk, talk, talk. Why? Because that is rarely what Jesus did.

Anyone who teaches the Jesus way must engage the learner. The next time you take the opportunity to teach Jesus' way, take His message and wrap it in a unique, unexpected, vivid way. Never, *never* make the message boring. It is not just the content, not just the class, but also how you deliver the message to the marketplace that matters. You and other teachers in your church's teaching ministry will be teaching like Jesus when the message gets to the marketplace with full power and impact and life change.

The Writers

Ron Brown is Ministry Design Specialist in the Sunday School/FAITH Ministry Department, where he is involved in the development of resources for general Sunday School leaders. He is a member of Pleasant Heights Baptist Church, Columbia Tennessee, where through various staff and volunteer roles he has been a leader in Sunday School ministry. Ron and his wife, Connie, are parents of two adult children, and have discovered the joys of being grandparents to William Keith Lewis. Ron has been a pastor and minister of education and is a 13-year employee of LifeWay Christian Resources.

Jay Johnston serves as Director of the Sunday School/FAITH Ministry Department, Sunday School Group. He is married to Jerilyn and they have two sons, John and Jody. He is actively involved in First Baptist Church of Hendersonville, Tennessee, where he serves as a Sunday School leader, FAITH Team Leader, and member of the Missions Committee. Previously he served in the Discipleship and Family Group at LifeWay Christian Resources and on church staffs in Louisiana, Florida, and Tennessee.

Bruce Wilkinson is founder and president of Walk Thru the Bible Ministries, Inc., in Atlanta, Georgia. Dr. Wilkinson is an internationally respected and highly sought-after Bible teacher. His writings and messages on audio and video are used throughout the world to encourage, challenge, and equip teachers for life-changing ministry. Dr. Wilkinson is the author of several best-selling resources for teachers and other leaders, including *The 7 Laws of the Learner, Teaching with Style,* and *The 3 Chairs.* In addition to writing the Introduction for *Teaching the Jesus Way: Building a Transformational Teaching Ministry,* Dr. Wilkinson delivers five messages on the videocassette that is included in the *Teaching the Jesus Way: Building a Transformational Teaching Ministry Leader Training Pack.*

Sunday School is the foundational strategy in a local church for leading people to faith in the Lord Jesus Christ and for building Great Commission Christians through Bible study groups that engage people in evangelism, discipleship, fellowship, ministry, and worship.

Spiritual transformation is God's work of changing a believer into the likeness of Jesus by creating a new identity in Christ and by empowering a lifelong relationship of love, trust, and obedience to glorify God.

He Was His Father's Son. Who Are You?

"You address me as 'Teacher' and 'Master,' and rightly so. That is what I am" (John 13:13). Of the several ways Jesus was addressed, the title *teacher* or *rabbi,* meaning one who taught with authority, was the title given to Him most frequently. Apparently, it was a title He accepted, for He affirmed His disciples' (learners') use of it and their recognition that He was, literally, "the teacher." His *mind-set* reflected His knowledge of who He was, contributing to His effectiveness and power.

As Teacher, Jesus had subject matter to teach. Therefore, He sought out learners. It was imperative that they learn, not just with the head but with the heart. As Teacher, Jesus would not just talk the lesson; He would be the lesson. Jesus "prepared" Himself to teach.

Because He was an effective teacher, He employed a variety of methods to get the attention of His learners, to convey information to them, and to challenge them to consider its meaning and allow themselves to be changed by it. As Teacher, He understood the value and benefit of knowing His learners. In fact, He knew them better than they knew themselves. Because of this relationship, He could teach them with greater purpose.

Matthew recognized a definite pattern in Jesus' ministry methodology, with teaching being a major component. "Jesus went throughout Galilee, teaching in their synagogues, preaching the good news of the kingdom, and healing every disease and sickness among the people" (Matt. 4:23, NIV; also see 9:35). Teaching pervaded all that He did.

His preaching, as does all good preaching, was filled with sound teaching. His healing, while motivated by His compassion for those in need, provided a vehicle for teaching truth. Indeed, all of His miracles had teaching at their heart.

Jesus' purpose for teaching was greater than presenting a plethora of facts to be intellectually accumulated or absorbed by His learners. His interest was not that His learners would simply be able to repeat certain information back to Him. Instead, Jesus taught the truth of God's Word so that those who heard it might be transformed.

Yes, they would have to hear it, intellectually process it, intentionally decide to commit themselves to it, and willingly submit themselves to the Holy Spirit who was at work through it. Even so, the objective of it all was that lives be changed. His goal for all His followers—those who followed Him in His earthly ministry as well as all who would follow later—was that they might be focused on becoming "fully developed within and without, fully alive like Christ" (Eph. 4:13).

All Christian ministry is an extension of Christ's ministry. Because teaching was a vital dimension of Jesus' ministry, it must be included in the ministry plan of His church, universally speaking and in every local expression. That He intended it to be this way can be realized by looking to the Great Commission. In the commission to His followers to make disciples, teaching is included as part of the plan for achieving that goal. Apparently His disciples took that charge seriously, for teaching became an important part of the corporate ministry of the early church, as seen in the practices described in Acts 2:42-47.

Teaching was an important part of individual ministries, too. Stephen included a didactic element in his lengthy discourse before the Sanhedrin (Acts 7). Philip explained Scripture to the Ethiopian who confessed he did not understand what he had been reading (Acts 8:30-31,35). Even the preacher Paul included teaching in his ministry and exhorted young protégés like Timothy and Titus to take teaching seriously (Acts 17:2-3; 20:20; 1 Tim. 1:3-11; 4:11-15; Titus 2).

But it all goes back to Jesus. Teaching, as an essential dimension of His ministry, was an expression of His commitment to God, His Father, and a means of carrying out the larger mission to which He had been called.

Jesus knew who He was. He was His Father's Son. It was that awareness that established the parameters for His entire life.

He Was His Father's Son

Look at two instances in Jesus' life that shaped His understanding of who He was and that placed His teaching—indeed, His entire life—in the context of divine calling.

Sensing a Call

Jesus' birth was surrounded with the glory, majesty, and purpose of God. Mary treasured it all, likely with the special ability that only a mother can realize (Luke 2:19; also see v. 51). How much did she tell the child Jesus in His growing-up years? With childlike curiosity, did Jesus ask about the family's past and especially about His own birth? It is intriguing to think about Jesus as a child: What was He like? Was He different from other children? How much did He know about Himself? Did He have any ideas about His mission in life? Most, if not all, of our answers to these and similar questions would be speculation.

We do have a story recorded only by Luke in which Jesus, as a 12-year-old boy, travels to Jerusalem with His family for Passover (Luke 2:41-51). It is the only bit of information we have about Jesus as a child aside from the birth narratives and the comprehensive statements that "the child grew strong in body and wise in spirit. And the grace of God was on him" (2:40; also see v. 52). The story of Jesus in the temple is an important passage of Scripture because it includes His first recorded words. And powerful words they were, too, because of the insight they provide into His own perception of who He was and the purpose of His life.

Jesus accompanied Mary and Joseph to Jerusalem for Passover. Likely, this was not the first time Jesus had been to Jerusalem for this holy observance, because Mary and Joseph went annually (Luke 2:41). Joseph went in part to fulfill a religious requirement. Mary probably went along as an act of devotion and to be with her family. However, Jesus' attendance this particular year differed in that He went as bar mitzvah, a "son of the law." He was at the age to enter into the privileges and responsibilities of an Israelite male. According to the law every male was to attend the three great feasts: Passover, Pentecost, and Tabernacles. After the Exile these requirements were not enforced and a choice could be made. Passover, regarded as the most solemn and important of the feasts, was frequently the feast of choice.

After the week of festival was over, Mary and Joseph joined a company of fellow travelers to return to their villages in Galilee. They assumed Jesus was with them as part of the traveling party. Only at the end of the day did they discover His absence. After searching for Him among their companions, the distraught parents returned to Jerusalem. Following what surely were three frantic days of searching, Mary and Joseph found the Boy engaged in dialogue with the rabbis in the temple courts. In response to His mother's anxious rebuke, Jesus said, "Why were you looking for me? Didn't you know that I had to be here, dealing with the things of my Father?" (v. 49). (Luke did not provide the object noun. Various translators insert the words *house, business,* or *things.)*

Regardless of the word supplied, Jesus was expressing His awareness of a special relationship to God. Jesus not only was legally a "son of the law," He perceived He was the Son of the Father. At least in part, He sensed the significant mission and calling that would shape His life.

Even so, Jesus returned to Nazareth, was subject to the guidance and instruction of His parents, was influenced by the conditions of His life situation, and worked and lived the rigorous lifestyle of a carpenter. These were not wasted years, for He grew physically, socially, and spiritually. He was being prepared to do what the Heavenly Father had sent Him to be and to do.

Affirming His Call

As a young adult, around 30 years of age, Jesus embarked on a ministry that would bring a sense of fulfillment to His calling. Why at that time? Perhaps the best explanation can be found only in that this was God's timing. But it should not escape us that Jesus now was prepared by the physical, social, and spiritual growth that had taken place in His life. Because He had matured physically, He was prepared for the rigorous demands of His itinerant ministry. His social maturity prepared Him to know how to encounter people of all stations and relate to people in all situations in life. His spiritual maturity increased His understanding of what He was about, of the scope of His call, of the unusual depth of relationship He had with God, who was His Father.

Then one day, with no explanation and certainly no fanfare, Jesus came to John the Baptizer requesting baptism at the hands of this strange messenger from God. Out of true humility, John resisted. Jesus, however, persisted, saying, "Do it. God's work, putting things right all these centuries, is coming together right now in this baptism" (Matt. 3:15). John was convinced and consented.

As Jesus came up out of the water, heaven provided a phenomenal display. The Spirit of God, descending from heaven like a dove gliding gracefully through the sky, came upon Jesus. A heavenly voice declared, "This is my Son, chosen and marked by my love; delight of my life" (v. 17). This display affirmed to Jesus the call of His Father.

He was the Father's Son. And as the Son, He must do the things of His Father's business. What were those things? This display from heaven gives insight into the ministry that lay before Jesus.

His endowment with the Spirit attested that His calling was to a spiritual purpose. This anointing of the Spirit constituted the anointing of Jesus as the Christ (Greek) or Messiah (Hebrew) of God. By this experience the words of the prophets were being fulfilled (Isa. 11:1-2).

The Spirit's coming upon Jesus was a confirmation of John's testimony. Through Jesus' baptism experience God declared that Jesus was the promised Messiah. God equipped and confirmed Jesus for His work and consecrated Him as the Messiah. The presence of the dove affirmed that the Holy Spirit empowered Jesus for His mission as the Messiah.

To accomplish what He was being called to accomplish could

not be done with human strength; He would need divine power. To know what He was to do would require more than human knowledge or insight; He would need wisdom from on high. The nature of the work He was to be about was a heavenly work. It could not be achieved through existing entities, institutions, or people of influence. Hence, the Spirit came upon Him.

Also part of the phenomenal display from heaven was a voice. The voice was the voice of God. The words God spoke were from Psalm 2:7, part of a royal psalm in which the reign of God's anointed was proclaimed, and Isaiah 42:1-6, which presents the first of the prophecies about a Suffering Servant. Taken together, the images presented in the words of the Voice was God's way of declaring that Jesus was His Anointed who would reign through suffering. That Jesus understood that soon would become clear.

From those baptismal waters Jesus arose with the appointment, approval, and affirmation that eliminated any hesitation concerning His call. He accepted His mission and with Holy Spirit endowment walked from those waters to live out His calling. Perhaps more than once when He faced intense opposition or was tempted to alter His mission, Jesus was encouraged to continue on by His own conviction that He "had to be here, dealing with the things of my Father," and the indelible memory of His Father's own words, "This is my Son, chosen and marked by my love."

One way Jesus carried out His calling was through teaching. People were accustomed to teachers and teaching in synagogue worship. In fact, Jesus inaugurated His public ministry by teaching in the synagogues of Galilee. His teaching captured the attention of people. Some were infuriated at the content, like the people in his hometown synagogue of Nazareth (Luke 4:16-30); others were amazed at what they heard—at both the content of His teaching and the authority with which He taught (Mark 1:21-28).

Jesus would not evaluate His effectiveness in teaching on the basis of His popularity with people, however. He came to do the will of His Father, and He would be faithful to His calling. Other concerns were secondary. In that, Jesus becomes a model for us all.

Whose Child Are You?

As a general Sunday School leader, you have a primary leadership role in the development of an effective Sunday School ministry in your church. If Sunday School is your church's foundational strategy, then your influence also will be felt in the broader scope of your church's life and ministry. Therefore, your position of leadership is not to be regarded lightly. It must be approached with conviction about who you are as God's child, an understanding of your life in the context of Kingdom service, and an abiding sense of a divine calling.

You Are a Child of God

That assertion is true if you have a personal relationship with God through Jesus Christ. God in His love and through Jesus Christ has made it possible for us to be children of God (John 1:12: 1 John 3:1-2). We may want to assume that relationship exists in the lives of those who serve in church ministry, yet it is too vital to rely only on an assumption. No person can serve the Lord with authenticity who does not in fact and through experience know Him as Lord and Savior. Therefore, affirm that relationship in your own life. Examine the scope, depth, quality, and reality of your relationship with Him. Build upon it so that you may be the leader God, as your Heavenly Father, wants you to be.

Furthermore, in enlisting coworkers, allow them an opportunity to give witness to their own relationship with God in Christ. If our ministry is to be a spiritually transforming ministry, then each person involved in it must know the reality of that transformation personally, not just theoretically.

God Is at Work in Your Life

As a general leader, you are a leader of leaders—the several other persons who are essential to effective Sunday School ministry. Most of those leaders will lead through the exercise of a teaching role in a class or department. To develop a Sunday School ministry with a focus on transformational teaching will require that they, too, know who they are as God's children, understand their lives in the context of kingdom service, and have a sense of divine calling. Furthermore, it will require teachers/leaders who are motivated and empowered not by obligation to a church program, ministry staff, a single leader, or enlistment process but by their relationship with God as Father and the indwelling presence of His Holy Spirit. Part of your role is to model before them what all that means and to challenge and encourage them in their own spiritual progression at each point.

Reflecting on the earlier instances in the life of Jesus as background, evaluate your own service as a Sunday School general leader. Use the following questions to guide you in your evaluation. Record your responses in the space provided or on additional sheets of paper.

How Has God Been at Work in Your Life?

In taking a spiritual inventory, Henry Blackaby, an author of *Experiencing God: Knowing and Doing the Will of God*, stated he found it helpful to look back over his life to see how God had directed his life according to His holy purpose. In doing so, he identified "spiritual markers," times of transition, decision, or direction when he clearly knew God had guided him. When he was facing a decision about God's future direction, Blackaby used these spiritual markers to help him see God's perspective for his past and present. He then evaluated future options to see which was most consistent with what God already was doing in his life.[1]

Look back at stories from the life of Jesus. Do you see how these few events could be identified as "spiritual markers" in His life?

• Learning from His mother the events surrounding His birth sparked Jesus' awareness of His special relationship with the Father.

• The dialogue with the rabbis in the temple further stimulated Jesus' concept of who He was and what He was about and provided the first known instance of giving expression to it.

• The ongoing influence and instruction by His parents provided foundational support for the ministry upon which He would embark.

• Jesus' physical, spiritual, and social maturing in the context of His family and community equipped Him for His ultimate mission.

• John the Baptizer became a key person in the initial stages of Jesus' ministry.

• Jesus' baptism was a high spiritual moment that offered affirmation to His self-identity and purpose for life and endowed Him for His calling.

• Jesus' familiarity with Scripture gave increased meaning to the words spoken by the voice of God at His baptism.

Now look back at your own life. Consider drawing a timeline for your life. Designate with a (x) on the timeline the spiritual markers you identify.

How did your family (you define who that is) positively or negatively influence your spiritual awareness and development as a child?

Recall your earliest recollection of a "church" experience. What made that a memorable moment for you?

Name a key person or two in your life who encouraged you spiritually and helped you discern God's purpose for you. What did those persons do to encourage or help you?

Think about a high spiritual moment you have had in your life. What made it meaningful? How has it contributed to your self-identity and prepared you for the service you are doing presently?

Give thanks to Jesus for your life as a leader and for how He has brought you this far. Acknowledge your desire to continue to glorify God as a leader.

Who Is Your Leadership Model?

For the Christian no other model need exist for leadership than Jesus Christ. He models kingdom leadership. "A kingdom leader can be defined as a person called by God to follow Christ in a life of discipleship, utilizing the leadership gifts given by the Holy Spirit to lead the church in carrying out the Great Commission for the purpose of expanding the kingdom of God."[2] As a general Sunday School leader, that definition should define what you are about and guide you as you develop others who are part of the Sunday School ministry leadership team.

One expression of kingdom leadership is servant leadership. All service is not leadership, but all leadership ought to be service. "The call is clear: the Christian leader is a person who has experienced the love of God and his grace, who projects the outward expression of this love toward others not for gain or fame or influence but with a free and happy will."[3] Jesus Himself becomes a model for the person who has been called to serve through leadership.

Those terms—*service* and *leadership*—seem incongruent—and

they are when measured against a world standard. The world standard describes leaders in much more aggressive terminology— causing us, for example, to think of leaders as "bosses."

Jesus challenged that concept in various conversations with His disciples about what constitutes greatness. He reminded them that the boss style of leadership was common practice in the Gentile culture (a culture few would want to emulate in other areas of life). What Jesus expected and modeled was a leadership style characterized by service to God and others (Mark 10:42-45; John 13:3-16).

Think again about the phenomenon associated with Jesus' baptism, especially the words of the voice from heaven. Those words affirmed His call as Messiah, the Father's business He sensed even as a young man. But those words also included a reference to the Suffering Servant (Isa. 42:1-9). Jesus would lead as Messiah, but as a servant Messiah. Just as servant leadership is an unusual combination for us, Servant Messiah was an unheard-of concept for Jesus' day. Yet that was His calling.

For a more complete understanding of the New Testament concept of servant leadership as practiced and modeled by Jesus, study the resource *Jesus on Leadership: Becoming a Servant Leader,* by C. Gene Wilkes. In that volume Wilkes describes the servant-leadership model:

> Leadership in the kingdom of God is different from leadership in the world. It is still leadership, but those who lead in the kingdom of God look very different from those who lead by the world's standards. Life under the lordship of Christ has different values than life under the lordship of self. Therefore, kingdom leaders are people who lead like Jesus. They act differently than leaders trained by the world. Kingdom leaders are servant leaders because they follow Jesus, who 'did not come to be served, but to serve' (Mark 10:45).[4]

The ultimate model of servant leadership is Jesus. Using Jesus as the model, Wilkes identifies "Seven Principles of Servant Leadership."[5]

1. Servant leaders humble themselves and wait for God to exalt them (Luke 14:7-11).

2. Servant leaders follow Jesus rather than seek a position (Mark 10:32-40).

3. Servant leaders give up personal rights to find greatness in service to others (Mark 10:41-45).

4. Servant leaders can risk serving others because they trust God is in control of their lives (John 13:3).

5. Servant leaders take up Jesus' towel of servanthood to meet the needs of others (John 13:4-11).

6. Servant leaders share their responsibility and authority with others to meet a greater need (Acts 6:1-6).

7. Servant leaders multiply their leadership by empowering others to lead (Ex. 18:17-23).

 Do these principles find expression in your ministry? Write a sentence that describes how each of these principles finds expression in your ministry as a general Sunday School leader.

1.

2.

3.

4.

5.

6.

7.

What "Moved" You to Accept Your Leadership Role?

From the instances cited earlier and your awareness of the gospel story, what do you think moved Jesus to do what He had come to do? Make a list in the margins of this book.

People accept leadership roles for various reasons. Consider these. Check any that apply to you. Certainly you may be moved by more than one factor.

❐ *Obligation.* A person may feel a sense of responsibility to accept a position by virtue of being a church member. This does not mean the person has a commitment to what he is doing.

❐ *Guilt.* A person may accept a leadership role because not to do so makes her feel she has done something wrong.

❐ *Personal need.* A person, for example someone struggling to find a stronger sense of self-worth, may accept a responsibility as a way of trying to restore some sense of pride in who he is.

❐ *Ego.* Someone may want to serve in a leadership position because he enjoys being in front of other people and benefits from the affirmation he receives from them.

❐ *Commitment to service.* Somewhat different from obligation, which may lack commitment, this person has a strong inner conviction that drives her to serve.

❐ *Godly desire.* This person desires to serve not for what he gains personally but because of a desire rooted in his relationship with God.

❐ *The enjoyment of using skills and talents.* An individual may assume a place of service because she clearly possess the skills and talents to do the job and enjoys using them in positive ways.

❐ *Love.* The greatest motivation for service (2 Cor. 5:14), this person loves God and loves his neighbor. That love is expressed in action.

❐ *Divine calling.* This does not exclude commitment to service, godly desire, enjoying the use of skills and talents, and love as motives for service. A divine calling is the culmination of those motivators to a particular place of service as a person has a clear and definite sense that God wants him in that place.

Has God Called You?

This becomes the pivotal question to ask yourself and to pose to others you enlist to lead in Sunday School ministry: *Has God called you to this place of service?* None of the motivations listed earlier are complete without a sense of call from God.

We also want leaders to be qualified for the role they accept. We tend to emphasize qualifications based on the skills and knowledge a person possesses. For example, we want a leader to have relational, organizational, and planning skills, to name a few. We want a leader to know his abilities, skills, and limitations; the abilities, skills, and limitations of those whom he is leading, the purpose of the group or organization; the way the group does its work; and the vision for the future. These qualifications are valuable, so we do well to look for people who are skilled and knowledgeable.

However, the most essential qualification for any ministry leader—outside of a personal, saving relationship with God through Jesus Christ—is a sense of call. No matter how competent, knowledgeable, or skilled, a person who tries to lead without a call from God will be lacking the dynamic power that God provides those whom He selects for His work.

Unfortunately, in the local church we too often have thought of "call" as an experience unique to the pastor, other vocational staff ministers, and missionaries. While the concept of call is and ought to be valid for each of those ministry areas, the experience of call ought not to be limited to them. Traditionally we have allowed this idea of a called ministry to result in a dichotomy of clergy and laity. We may think of the clergy as "called;" the laity on the other hand are "enlisted" or selected according to some internal process or practice agreed upon by a church. Such a difference is difficult to justify by New Testament standards.

For one example, look at some words in First Peter, a letter addressed to believers who were scattered in various regions. Peter gave them words of assurance and challenge by reminding them, "God the Father has his eye on each of you, and has determined by the work of the Spirit to keep you obedient through the sacrifice of Jesus" (1:2). Later he would add: "You are the ones chosen by God, chosen for the high calling of priestly work, chosen to be a holy people, God's instruments to do his work and speak out for him, to tell others of the night-and-day difference he made for you—from nothing to something, from rejected to accepted" (1 Pet. 2:9). Notice the strong emphasis on having been selected or chosen. And remember, his words were directed at believers, not a select group of professionals in religion.

Do you see the pattern here? At Jesus' baptism the Spirit descended on Him, sanctifying Him or setting Him aside for God's holy purpose of "putting things right" (Matt. 3:14). Peter himself was immersed in the Spirit (Acts 2; 4:8) and declared that he could not help but speak of what he had seen and heard in Jesus (see Acts 4:12,19-20). Then Peter reminds his readers they had been set aside by the Spirit to obey Jesus Christ. The pattern does not end. We too have been endowed with the Spirit for obedience to Christ (Matt. 28:18-20; John 20:22-23; Acts 1:8). That is what it means to be called.

 In assessing your ministry as a Sunday School leader, underline the statements with which you agree. If you disagree, offer your perspective by writing an answer to the questions.

1. *Calls from God are not issued at random, but each person is specifically chosen and called by God for His purpose.* Describe your own sense of call to your leadership role. How does the leadership role you have fit into the larger purpose you perceive God has for your life?

2. *God equips those whom He calls.* Describe how God has prepared and equipped you for your leadership position. Think about the spiritual gifts He has given you and the other formal and informal preparations in your life that have brought you to where you are now. Were those incidental occurrences, or do you see them in light of the sovereign plan and purpose of God?

3. *In calling a person to service, God most desires the person, not what the person can do.* What does that say about how God looks at us?

4. *Before a person can do what God has called him to do, he must be what God wants him to be.* Our being in Christ is a spiritual work of transformation. How has the Lord changed you?

5. *God has expectations of those whom He calls: faithfulness, obedience, sacrifice, service, influence, commitment, just to name a few.* Assess how you are fulfilling these expectations as a leader. In what ways can you apply yourself to be more of what God expects? How can you begin to do it?

6. *Consistent communion with God is critical to effectiveness in living out one's calling from God.* A person cannot be faithful to God's calling if he or she never talks to God about it. Did you talk to the Lord today about the calling He has on your life? Pause, giving thanks to the Lord for your calling. If you are struggling at this point, intentionally seek God in that struggle.

Lead Teachers to Reflect on Their Call from God

The focus of this book is on teaching—transformational teaching. That concept will be explained as we continue. Essentially it is teaching the Bible to the end that people be transformed, changed, converted by an encounter with God through Jesus Christ in the power of His Holy Spirit. Purpose is the distinctive that separates teaching in Sunday School ministry and the teaching that takes place in most other settings. Purpose is what makes a Sunday School Bible study teacher different than most other teachers.

Lucien Coleman drew upon some words by Floyd Filson to accent that difference. Those words are appropriate here.

> We may think of a teacher as an instructor in a technical skill, or in some cultural or business interest, or in an academic atmosphere as a transmitter of information, a guide, or a trainer. These conceptions are totally foreign to the biblical ideal for the teacher. In the biblical view, the teacher is called of God to aid men in understanding the meaning of life in a God-centered world, and to guide them in finding, facing, and fulfilling the divine will.[6]

A Sunday School ministry that aims to teach for spiritual transformation requires an unusual kind of teacher. The fundamental requirement is that the person is teaching from a sense of call, the same sense of call realized by Jesus, testified to in the life of your pastor; and that is the driving force in your own leadership. One of the most important assignments you have as a general Sunday School leader who desires to build a Sunday School ministry characterized by transformational teaching is to gather a teaching and leadership team who is called of God.

The enlistment process you use as a general leader needs to function from the point of seeking out the called, not filling positions. It takes more time to enlist a person from the point of call, but the results are worth the time investment.

Properly enlisting a person is the first step toward good leadership. The objective of the enlistment process is to support someone in understanding the call of God relative to a specific leadership need and his/her own spiritual gifts. Let God do the calling; the results will be more fulfilling for everyone.

- Pray for God to lead you to the one person whom He wants you to enlist for a position. You already have identified potential leaders who have specific gifts. Pray over this list and ask God to select a person for the position. As you pray, ask God to start moving in the person's heart.

- Make an appointment to visit with the prospective leader. Schedule the appointment for the time and place most convenient for the person to be enlisted. Often this will be in the person's home. Be sure to be on time. Explain up front why you want to visit. Let the person know you feel God is leading you in a particular direction and that you want to discuss that leading with him.

- Provide the prospective leader with a written list of duties for the position you are asking her to consider. Make sure the list includes all expectations, such as participation in visitation, leadership meetings, witness training, and so forth.

- Inform the prospective leader of the term of service intended. In most cases, except when someone is enlisted to fill a vacancy during the year, the term of service would be one year. Indicate also that service for this year is no guarantee of being in that position next year. Explain that your goal is to give every person an opportunity to serve God in a position that makes best use of his/her talents and spiritual gifts.

- Provide the prospective leader with copies of essential materials to help in doing the work. Leader and member Bible study materials, resource kits, maps, and information about other available resources should be provided. If the prospective leader declines to serve, you can ask him to return the materials.

• Give the individual adequate time to discuss with you what is expected of leaders serving in this position. Encourage the prospective leader to ask questions now, but also provide your telephone number for contact later when other questions arise. Be honest. The prospective leader has the right to know as much as possible about the responsibilities.

• Explain what support systems are available and who will be working in similar capacities. One way for the individual to discover what the job entails is to observe in that age group. Encourage department leaders to be ready on an ongoing basis to have prospective workers observe, and then inform them prior to a specific person's visit. Age-group leaders who can share the joys and opportunities of service can help a prospective worker make an informed decision.

• Ask the prospective leader to pray about the position, and promise to do the same. Pray, giving thanks for whatever answer will be given and trusting that both you and the prospective worker have sought God in this process. The objective is for both of you to discern God's direction for the situation.

• Set a time (usually a week later) to contact the person for a decision. Setting a time to call back takes pressure off the person from feeling a decision must be given immediately.
   Accept the person's answer. Do not try to force the person to accept responsibilities he or she really does not want to accept. If the person accepts the position, provide additional details about planning, worker enlistment, and training.

• If a new leader is responsible for enlisting others, train him to use the same techniques that you modeled.

My Commitment as a Sunday School Leader

(This commitment is made between you and God and no one else. After prayerful consideration, sign your name. Keep the commitment form in your Bible as a reminder throughout the year.)

Because I feel called by God, I, _____, make this commitment as a Sunday School leader in my church.

As a Sunday School leader, I am committed to:

God in Christ
- I have a personal relationship with Jesus Christ that I desire to model for others.
- I enjoy studying the Bible, pray regularly, and desire to grow in my faith and commitment to Him.

Our Church
- I worship regularly with our church family.
- I support the Lord's work in the total church ministry by giving of my time, talents, and money.

My Class Members and Prospects
- I enjoy (preschoolers) (children) (youth) (young adults) (adults) and desire for them to know of God's love and purpose for their lives.
- I will take the necessary time to prepare, incorporating my own God-given gifts into each session.
- I will care for my members and prospects individually, through prayer, telephone calls, cards, and ministry actions.
- I will follow up with mailings, cards, or visits to absentees and prospects.
- I will be faithful in attendance, arriving at least 15 minutes before the session begins.
- If I must be absent, I will secure a replacement and notify my department or division director as soon as possible.
- I will participate in at least one training event during the year to improve my teaching skills.

The Teaching Team
- I will participate in scheduled leadership team meetings.
- I will communicate regularly with the other leaders on my team.

Signed _____ Date _____

Lead Teachers to Respond with a Commitment

How, then, should a person respond to the call to teach? It is a serious call, one which we are warned in Scripture not to take lightly (Jas. 3:1). Like every call from God, it demands a commitment. The commitment is multidimensional. See page 33 for a "My Commitment" worksheet that could be used as part of the enlistment process for selecting leaders in Sunday School ministry. Consider these areas of commitment.

A Commitment to God

• A Sunday School leader has a vital, personal relationship with Jesus Christ that he or she desires to model for others.
• A Sunday School leader studies the Bible consistently, prays regularly, and desires to grow in faith and commitment to Him.

A Commitment to the Church

• A Sunday School leader worships regularly with his or her church family.
• A Sunday School leader supports the Lord's kingdom work by giving of his or her time, talents, and money.

Using the above statements, how do you evaluate the commitment exhibited by the Sunday School leaders in your church? Identify those areas that need attention. Determine why a commitment to that area is important to living out the call as a Sunday School leader.

A Commitment to Class Members and Prospects

• A Sunday School leader enjoys the age group with which he or she works and desires for them to know of God's love and purpose for their lives.

• A Sunday School leader takes the necessary time to prepare, incorporating his or her own God-given gifts into each session.

• A Sunday School leader cares for members and prospects individually, through prayer, telephone calls, cards, and ministry actions.

• A Sunday School leader follows up with mailings, cards, or visits to absentees and prospects.

• A Sunday School leader is faithful in attendance, arriving at least 15 minutes before the session begins.

• When he or she must be absent, a Sunday School leader will secure a replacement and notify the department or division director as soon as possible.

• A Sunday School leader participates in at least one training event during the year to improve his or her teaching skills.

A Commitment to the Teaching Team

• A Sunday School leader participates in scheduled leadership meetings.

• A Sunday School leader communicates regularly with the other leaders on the team.

How is commitment important to the effectiveness of Sunday School ministry?

Of course, because of the free will that God gave us as part of our nature not everyone responds positively or immediately to His call. Several reasons may be offered by an individual for saying no to a call from God, and excuses may be given for a delay in giving a positive response. Here are a few examples from biblical history.

- Moses said that he was slow of speech and just could not handle the serious task to which God called him (Ex. 4:10, 13).
- Gideon's excuse when called of God was, "I am the least in my family" (Judg. 6:15, NIV).
- Isaiah saw the Lord and heard His call, but responded: "Woe to me! . . . For I am a man of unclean lips, and I live among a people of unclean lips" (Isa. 6:5a, NIV).

Some may hesitate to respond to the call to teach because they see teaching as a special task that only a few should even attempt. While the New Testament indicates that the responsibility for teaching was delegated to some church leaders (Eph. 4:11-13), the privilege of teaching was not limited to official leaders. Passages like Colossians 3:16 suggest that the teaching function be shared by all.

But how about the warning issued by James: "Don't be in any rush to become teachers, my friends. Teaching is highly responsible work. Teachers are held to the strictest standards. And none of us are perfectly qualified" (Jas. 3:1-2a). Who can meet that kind of demand?

Similarly, none of us wants to be described as a people who "set themselves up as experts on religious issues, but haven't the remotest idea of what they are holding forth with such imposing eloquence" (1 Tim. 1:7). Teaching is too serious a responsibility, too great a privilege, and too important to kingdom work to be entrusted to those who are not prepared, not committed, and not called to it.

That is why a divinely called-out staff of teachers is so vital to Sunday School ministry. To those who know the Lord personally and intimately, the call to teach is a heavenly calling that cannot be disobeyed (Acts 26:19). It is not something desired for selfish reasons, which was James' concern. It is a summons to join in the work of God who, although all-powerful and all-knowing, has determined in His sovereign will to call out human beings as conduits through which His message of redemption is transmitted.

As a general Sunday School ministry leader, offer a challenge to Sunday School teachers to hear and heed the call of God, to make that the foremost reason for service. Lead them to an awareness of God's need for interpreters of His message of salvation and abundant life. Help them see their teaching positions not as staff to a program or elements of an organization. Rather, lead them to see themselves as a people with a fresh vision of God, a people who cannot help but say with Isaiah, "Here am I. Send me" (Isa. 6:5, NIV). "Christian teaching will once again regain the preeminence it enjoyed in the New Testament when churches come to regard the selection of teachers as 'calling out the called,' rather than a coaxing of the recalcitrant."[7]

Remind Teachers Why We Teach

We have seen that the central command in the Great Commission is to "make disciples" (Matt. 28:19, NIV). Jesus gave a three-part plan for fulfilling the commission: "go," "baptizing," "teaching." All three parts are essential to Sunday School ministry: go to the people and share the gospel, assimilate them into the fellowship, and teach them to obey Jesus' commands. Therefore, one reason we teach people the Bible is obedience to the Lord's command.

If one word were to capture the goal for teaching people the Bible, that word might be *Christlikeness*. The goal of Bible study and biblical instruction is transformed lives that exhibit love for God and others (Matt. 22:37-40; 1 Tim. 1:5). Such lives glorify God because they are Christlike in nature (2 Cor. 3:18; Col. 3:16-17).

To accomplish this vision, leaders must model the truth that God transforms lives day-by-day. As teachers teach God's Word, they move beyond transferring biblical information and calling for discussions about application to walking with their learners in obedient, Christ-centered living.

As Jesus indicated in His prayer (John 17:17), it is God's Word that sanctifies—sets believers apart from the world for service to the world. Exposing God's Word to the hearts and minds of people, both lost and saved, so that they may be transformed in Christ is what Sunday School is all about.

The challenge of the Great Commission, the work of the kingdom, and a world in despair waits on those who hear the Lord's calling as their calling and who will make a positive, obedient response to be part of this important ministry of the church—teaching to change lives.

As a leader, what is *your* response to the Great Commission, the work of the kingdom, and a world that is waiting to hear?

End Notes

[1] Henry Blackaby and Claude V. King, *Experiencing God: How to Live the Full Adventure of Knowing and Doing the Will of God* (Nashville: Broadman & Holman Publishers, 1994), 124-125.

[2] Michael D. Miller, *Kingdom Leadership: A Call to Christ-Centered Leadership* (Nashville: Convention Press, 1996), 72.

[3] Bruce Grubbs, "Simon Peter: Shaped by a Powerful Model," *Leadership Profiles from Bible Personalities,* Ernest E. Mosley, compiler (Nashville: Broadman Press, 1979), 124.

[4] C. Gene Wilkes, *Jesus on Leadership: Becoming a Servant Leader* (Nashville: LifeWay Press, 1996), 8.

[5] Wilkes, see summary, cover page 4.

[6] Lucien E. Coleman, Jr., *Why the Church Must Teach* (Nashville: Broadman Press, 1984), 50.

[7] Ibid., 146.

He Knew What He Was About. What Are You About?

Jesus knew whose He was; therefore, He knew who He was. That made it possible for Him to know what He was about, what He was to be doing, and what He wanted to achieve.

In other words, Jesus' life and ministry was intentional and purposeful. His actions in life were deliberately directed to that end. He was focused on the *mission*.

He Knew What He Was About

To have a purpose is to have a clear and dominant sense of what one is seeking to accomplish. Purpose becomes the focus around which a life—whether an individual or an organization—is centered. Purpose provides stability, direction, and focus.

No one models the purpose-filled life better than Jesus. His purpose for coming dominated everything He did. As an agent of spiritual transformation and redemption, His purpose was to bring others into right relationship with God the Father. That same sense of purpose, which He began to realize as a boy, continued throughout His life, even in His death.

Consider this sampling of statements and actions that express in various ways what Jesus was about.

Why Jesus Came

He came to bring hope to those in despair. In His inaugural sermon at the synagogue in Nazareth, He identified Himself with the servant of hope described by the prophet Isaiah and declared Himself to be the fulfillment of Scripture (Luke 4:16-21). The eternal consequences of sin bring about great despair and hopelessness. Jesus came to enable us to be free from sin, alive with hope, and liberated from despair.

He came to reach out to sinners. When confronted by the Pharisees about His willingness to associate with societal outcasts, Jesus responded by saying that was why He had come: to call out sinners—those who were rejected by others—to the changed life. He had not come to call out the righteous—those who were already satisfied with themselves (Luke 5:32), for they would not hear Jesus anyway. Jesus came to declare God's love for sinners and His willingness to welcome them into His family.

He came to seek out and to save the lost. After a life-changing encounter with Zacchaeus, Jesus pointed to him as a model of why He had come: "The Son of Man came to find and restore the lost" (Luke 19:10). What had happened to Zacchaeus was possible for everyone. To be lost is to be separated from the place where one is secure. The greatest sense of lostness comes from being separated from God by sin. Jesus came to seek us out and save us from eternal lostness.

He came to ransom the captive. During a discussion in which Jesus' disciples were overly concerned with what they would attain, Jesus stated that He had come "to give away his life in exchange for many who are held hostage" (Mark 10:45). Many things hold people hostage. At the root of them all is sin. Hence, Jesus came to free us from sin by giving His own life.

He came to do the Father's will and work. In fact, doing the Father's will and work was that which nourished and energized Him. He told His disciples it was His food, a statement like several others that left them puzzled (John 4:31-34). The Lord does not desire that any perish in their sin but that all come to repentance by faith in Jesus (2 Pet. 3:9). That is one expression of the will of God and the work Jesus came to accomplish.

He came to make possible super-abundant living. Using the analogy of the shepherd, Jesus affirmed He had come for life in contrast to the thief who came for death and destruction (John 10:10). The thief is Satan. Jesus is the Good Shepherd. He came to give life that cannot be taken away (John 10:27-30).

He came to bring glory to God, His Father. Jesus felt confident He had done that. In His priestly prayer in the Garden just prior to His arrest, He said, "I glorified you on earth by completing down to the last detail what you assigned me to do . . . . I spelled out your character in detail to the men and women you gave me. . . . I have made your very being known to them—who you are and what you do" (John 17:4,6,26).

Those are just some statements that describe in various ways Jesus' purpose for coming and His devotion to it. He was committed to bringing all people into right relationship with God. He would not be turned away from accomplishing His purpose. He would "set his face to go to Jerusalem" (Luke 9:51, KJV) even when He knew that the cross awaited Him (Luke 9:22). He would give Himself to the end, so that with His dying breath He could say confidently, "It's done . . . complete" (John 19:30).

What Kind of Messiah Would He Be?

Even so, Jesus was not without challenge concerning His purpose and how He would accomplish His calling. Look at four instances in His life in which He was challenged to reconsider His mission, the purpose of His calling, or the results He was to achieve. Notice that by enduring these challenges to forsake who He was and what He was about, Jesus reaffirmed His relationship to the Father, reassessed the purpose of His ministry, and recommitted Himself to His kingdom mission.

The Challenge in the Wilderness

Jesus' baptismal event declared who He was and the kind of Messiah He would be. What approach would He take to accomplish His purpose of bringing others into a right relationship with God? The answer to that significant question would come in the wilderness.

All three synoptic Gospels tell about the wilderness testing Jesus faced following His baptism; albeit, Mark's account lacks any details. The temptations or tests were not immoral in nature. In fact, one thing that made the temptations so challenging was that there was nothing inherently bad in them. Yet they constituted serious challenges to Jesus. "The temptation was to take a short-cut to immediate goals yielding real benefactions or to employ the wrong means to achieve goals which at least in part represented valid human needs. But Jesus, who could offer only a narrow gate and an anguished way to his followers (Matt. 7:13-14), could choose no easy way for himself."[1]

We need not discount the intensity of this experience for Jesus. Don't get caught up in the erroneous speculation that Jesus could not have succumbed to the temptations anyway. We tend to do that out of our understanding that He is the holy, righteous Son of God. So He is, but that does not mean this experience lacked the anguish that is associated with deeply inward, spiritual struggle. Moreover, temptations that cannot be submitted to are not temptations at all. If Jesus did not face real temptations to which He could submit, then the entire story becomes a hypothetical situation.

No, Jesus faced actual challenges to the nature and scope of His call as Messiah. Would He avoid the difficult way, or would He choose a populist, spectacular, or self-serving approach?

One more observation before we look at the temptations. Notice that Satan introduced some of the temptations with the words, "If you are the Son of God" (Matt. 4:3,6, NIV). *If* could also be translated *since.* Both translations are valid. Did he employ these words as a tactic to raise doubt, or to lead Jesus to presume upon that relationship? More likely it was the latter. Jesus had settled the issue of Sonship. The question was what kind of Son He would be; would He be one who made demands of His Father or one who willingly submitted in obedience before Him? As Son, did Jesus not have the right to use the power and privilege that was His in the ways He wanted, or would He choose the greater good that sprang from obedience to the Father's will?

An economic approach.—The first temptation drew from Jesus' own hunger after spending extended time in prayer and fasting. The brown stones that covered the ground in the desert region would easily remind a hungry person of the brown loaves of round bread with which the people were familiar.

Human hunger is a basic need. People are determined and driven to satisfy that need. What if someone came along with the power to turn the stones, which were plentiful, into bread?

Certainly such a person would be well accepted and would earn the loyalty of the people. With that loyalty Jesus could lead them to the kingdom where the greater need of life could be met. Jesus rejected that approach, for first place in life must be given to spiritual need. "It takes more than bread to stay alive. It takes a steady stream of words from God's mouth" (Matt. 4:4).

A religious approach.—The second temptation drew on the intrigue of people with signs and wonders that were so much a part of their religious heritage. For Jesus to cast Himself from the pinnacle of the temple, which in itself was a pinnacle of religion in Jerusalem, and be spared harm by being caught mid-air by swarming angels would be a spectacular occurrence. Think of the attention it would garner. The people would be so impressed that Jesus had such command and influence with God and His angels, surely they would follow Him.

No, the spectacular, even with religious overtones, was not what the people needed. Jesus asserted, "Don't you dare test the Lord your God" (4:7). A religion that tests God is a sham. What is needed is a call to be a people of faith in a God who can be counted on but who is not to be presumed upon.

A political approach.—The third temptation drew upon the desire of the people that one day Israel would be freed from the domination of Rome and be restored as a ruling nation in the world. The long-expected messiah would rally the people and lead them to victory. If Jesus would compromise Himself and join in league with the powers of this world, He could succeed as Messiah. He could indeed build world kingdoms. Jesus rejected that approach as well, for His kingdom was not of this world. He declared, "Worship the Lord your God, and only him. Serve him with absolute single-heartedness" (4:10). Rather than enslave Himself to the powers of the world, Jesus would submit Himself to God His Father.

The Servant's approach.—Resisting these temptations, Jesus affirmed that He would choose the path of service and sacrifice. At the end of that path lay a cross. Upon picking up that cross, He would find a crown. In time God His Father would make Him to be "KING OF KINGS, LORD OF LORDS" (Rev. 19:16).

A Challenge by the Crowds

The tests Jesus faced in the desert wilderness may have ended, but not temptation. Luke alludes to continuing temptation by noting that "the Devil retreated temporarily, lying in wait for another opportunity" (4:13). More was to come, continuing to challenge Jesus at the point of His relationship to the Father, His kingdom mission, and His ministry's purpose.

John tells of Jesus' encounter with a crowd of people whom Jesus realized were eager to conscript Him as their king (John 6:15). It followed the miraculous feeding of the thousands at Jesus' hands by multiplying the few fishes and loaves. The devil was right. People would respond to miracles and bread. However, they won't stay, for when the bread is gone, so are they (6:66-67).

To combat this challenge, Jesus withdrew to the mountain alone. Yet, He was not alone. For although John does not say it explicitly, this likely was time for Jesus to spend time with His Father (see Matt. 14: 22-23; Mark 6:45-46). Once again Jesus reaffirmed His relationship as Son, recommitted Himself to His kingdom mission, and reassessed His ministry purpose. Once again, He determined to live out His calling.

A Challenge by One Closest to Him

One challenge to Jesus' faithfulness to His calling came from one of His closest followers: Simon Peter. During a respite from the press of the people and the demands of ministry, Jesus, ever the teacher, quizzed His disciples about the perceptions people had of Him. He then made the quiz more personal by asking for their understanding of who He was.

Simon Peter made the bold declaration, "You are the Christ, the

Messiah, the Son of the living God" (Matt. 16:16). How Jesus' heart must have leapt within, for that was what He would have them know. Jesus affirmed Simon Peter by saying, "God bless you, Simon, son of Jonah! You didn't get that answer out of books or from teachers. My Father in heaven, God himself, let you in on this secret of who I really am" (v. 17). Indeed, Peter's understanding was a spiritual revelation, not just human knowledge.

Jesus began to build on Peter's declaration to explain the implications of being Messiah. His words were a radical departure from the popular conception, especially the part about being killed. So much so that Simon Peter challenged Jesus: "Impossible, Master! That can never be!" (v. 22). What would Jesus do in this face of a challenge by one so close to Him? Would He forsake His relationship with the Father, His calling to kingdom mission, and the focus of His ministry? No, He would not. So clear was His calling that even to a close friend He said, "Peter, get out of my way. Satan, get lost. You have no idea how God works" (v. 23). Jesus' call was clear; His purpose was firm. He would not be turned back even by those closest to Him.

An Agonizing Challenge from Within

In Gethsemane Jesus once and for all agonized over His commitment to the Father's calling. The agony is described in intense terms by the Gospel writers (see Matt. 26:37-38; Mark 14:33-34; Luke 22:44). The "cup," probably a reference to His imminent suffering and death, was setting before Him. The natural inclination would be to shrink away from it, to refuse to take it to His lips. Jesus submitted that inclination to His greater desire to do His Father's will. He would be His Father's Son. He would accept His calling. He would achieve His kingdom mission. He would fulfill His purpose. And because He did, all people through faith in Him could be saved, transformed into His likeness. That was why He came (John 3:16-17,36). Without question, He knew what He was about.

What Are You About?

You and your church may be the proverbial beehive of activity. Many, perhaps most, churches are. But does all that activity move you toward fulfilling your kingdom mission. Even doing what is fascinating or popular may not help accomplish purpose. Those were the issues Jesus faced. They are not dissimilar to the issues you, your church, and its Sunday School ministry face. Don't be deceived.

A Parable of Misperception

Some leaders are like a man named Wahlstrom, in a story told by Alvin J. Lindgren and Norman Shawchuck. Wahlstrom was a mechanically minded man who enjoyed going to surplus sales and buying various electrical and engineering components. He dismantled the parts and put them back together in various, unusual configurations. Before long, he had a room in his house filled with different size wheels, bells, and lights.

The mechanism he developed was amazing. Upon entering the room, he could push a button and several small wheels would begin to turn. The various gears would mesh with each other until all around the room were wheels turning and whirring. When the last wheel went into motion, a light would begin flashing and then another, and another. Gradually the room was filled with a series of flashing lights. When the final light began flashing, a bell would start to ring. Each bell led to the ringing of another bell. By this time, Wahlstrom was standing in the middle of a room of whirring wheels, flashing lights, and ringing bells. Other people who saw it stood in awe.

One day a visitor to "Wahlstrom's Wonder," impressed by the mechanical display, said, "Mr. Wahlstrom this is really fascinating, but what does it do?" Wahlstrom explained, "Well, when you push the button the wheels turn, the lights flash, and the bells ring." The man replied, "Yes, I can see that, but what does it do?" And again Mr. Wahlstrom replied, "Well, you push a button, the wheels turn and . . ." Yes, but Mr. Wahlstrom, the questions still remain: What does it do? What function does it perform? Why does it exist? What does this wonder, fascinating and as popular as it had become, accomplish?[2]

As a Sunday School leader, you are responsible for leading out in developing a well-built, well-maintained, and vibrantly-effective Sunday School ministry. You will lead annual, monthly, and weekly planning. You will guide the development of an effective organization. You will encourage your church to secure the best possible equipment, space, and supplies. You will enlist a leadership team that is equally well-prepared and skilled. Alas, how sad to have all that in place but not to know what the purpose is; to be devoting all that energy in the wrong direction; or just to be like a display of wheels, lights, and bells that, in the end, do nothing.

Is Your Purpose Clear?

Ask most people the purpose of Sunday School, or what they are trying to achieve in Sunday School, and they are likely to respond with answers similar to these: "Teach the Bible," "Help people know more about the Bible," "Build up the fellowship," or possibly, "Build up the church." Each of those responses represents good things, but each only partially and incidentally represents the purpose of Sunday School.

Bill L. Taylor and Louis B. Hanks, national Sunday School leaders at LifeWay Christian Resources, challenged churches to rethink the purpose of Sunday School. In their book *Sunday School for a New Century* they wrote:

> While teaching-learning and caring fellowship both are essential, they often are focused toward people who have already been reached. Sunday School that focuses only on those who have been reached has lost sight of the church's primary responsibility—fulfilling the Great Commission.
>
> If Sunday School is to become more helpful to a church, classes and departments—the Bible study groups where the work is actually done—must break free from the tendency to focus inwardly. Members of the Bible study groups must be challenged

to serve Christ and follow His example. They must be organized for service, equipped for every good work, and mobilized for ministry.

For these things to happen, we need to rethink our understanding of Sunday School. It is not an educational entity. It is not a program or an organization. Sunday School is a strategy, a plan for doing the work of the church. It becomes foundational to everything we do.[3]

Think Through Your Understanding of Sunday School Ministry

As a Sunday School leader, how do you define Sunday School? Use the space below to write your own definition of Sunday School. Include in your definition at least three elements: What Sunday School is, why it exists, how it accomplishes its work. How is your definition or understanding of Sunday School influencing the leadership you are providing?

Is your definition of Sunday School one that is commonly accepted by other Sunday School leaders in your church? Do those who are members of the classes and departments in your church's Sunday School ministry generally accept it as well?

What can be done to ensure that you, other leaders, and members have a common understanding of what Sunday School is and why it exists as a ministry of your church?

Pray right now that God would begin working in the lives of Sunday School leaders for the purpose of bringing a common understanding of Sunday School ministry in your church.

1•5•4 Principle of Kingdom Growth

1

driving force

The Great Commission

5

essential functions

Evangelism
Discipleship
Fellowship
Ministry
Worship

4

results

Numerical Growth
Spiritual Growth
Ministries Expansion
Missions Advance

Rethinking and Redefining Sunday School

Sunday School is the foundational strategy in a local church for leading people to faith in the Lord Jesus Christ and for building Great Commission Christians through Bible study groups that engage people in evangelism, discipleship, fellowship, ministry, and worship.

Sunday School is foundational strategy. That is a new way of thinking about Sunday School. It is not one of many programs that are attached to an already overcrowded church schedule. It is not an organization we must continue to perpetuate out of commitment to longstanding tradition. It is not just an entity we point to with pride when we need to describe how large we are as a church.

What does it mean for Sunday School to be the "foundational strategy" in a local church? Simply stated, Sunday School is a strategy that guides people to come to know Jesus and then begin to deepen their lives in evangelism, discipleship, fellowship, ministry, and worship. Knowing Jesus and learning what it means to follow Jesus is a transforming—life-changing—experience. That is the goal of the teaching that takes place in the Bible study groups that are the vehicles for carrying out the strategy.

But Sunday School as strategy is not limited to a meeting time. It is always happening as its leaders prepare to lead people to encounter God's Word in Bible study groups committed to continue learning and living for Christ daily in all relationships, including the family.

Sunday School in the Kingdom Perspective

Jesus taught His followers to seek the kingdom of God as the priority of their lives (Matt. 6:33). The New Testament outlines five functions that reflect God's way of building His kingdom in the world through the local church: evangelism, discipleship, fellowship, ministry, and worship. Four kinds of growth result when a body of believers faithfully follows these essential functions: numerical growth, spiritual growth, ministries expansion, and missions advance. The 1·5·4 Principle—focused on 1 Great Commission, 5 church functions, and 4 results—is the driving force for Sunday School ministry and Bible study resources. (See the visual on p. 50.)

Five Strategic Sunday School Principles

Driven by a commitment to the Great Commission and building off a new understanding of Sunday School as foundational strategy, Sunday School will thrive in the new century as its leaders and learners participate in Bible study groups that are continually open to both believers and unbelievers. Five principles set the course.

The Principle of Foundational Evangelism.—Sunday School is the foundational evangelism strategy of the church. Because Sunday School provides ongoing, open Bible study groups that reproduce new groups, Sunday School is the best long-term approach for building a ministry environment for all age groups and the family. Sunday School aims to guide preschoolers and children toward conversion through foundational teaching. Sunday School encourages unsaved people to come to faith in Christ, assimilates new believers into the life of the church, and calls believers to lead others to Christ.

The Principle of Foundational Discipleship.—Knowing God through Jesus is the first step of discipleship. Sunday School as a strategy impacts people seven days a week, and open Bible study groups serve as a foundational step of discipleship. Through small groups—both classes and departments—Sunday School organizes people in such a way that individuals and families can participate in the comprehensive work of the church in evangelism, discipleship, fellowship, ministry, and worship. It encourages participants to strengthen their Christian faith by getting involved in other discipleship opportunities.

The Principle of Family Responsibility.—Sunday School operates as a supportive partner with parents, affirming the home as the center of biblical guidance. Through its resources, Sunday School is committed to help equip Christian parents, including single parents, to fulfill their responsibility as the primary Bible teachers and disciplers of their children. In addition, Sunday School will seek to nurture sound and healthy families and seek to lead non-Christian family members to Christ.

The Principle of Spiritual Transformation.—Sunday School engages learners in the biblical process of instruction that leads to spiritual transformation. Spiritual transformation is God's work of changing a believer into the likeness of Jesus by creating a new identity in Christ and by empowering a lifelong relationship of love, trust, and obedience to glorify God. By providing systematic Bible study, Sunday School calls upon believers to integrate the Bible's absolute truth into every area of life, thereby developing a biblical worldview. Sunday School also recognizes that Bible study is most effective when it occurs in the context of the learner's total life, especially family relationships, and when it considers the special needs, generational perspective, age and life-stage characteristics, and learning styles of the individual.

The Principle of Biblical Leadership.—Sunday School calls leaders to follow the biblical standard of leadership. Sunday School affirms the pastor as the primary leader in its ministry of building Great Commission Christians. Sunday School recognizes that the leader is the lesson in that every leader is accountable for being an authentic example of Christianity in personal living and producing new leaders for the ministries of the church. The main function of Sunday School leaders is to listen to God's voice through the Scriptures, discern God's message, integrate it into their lives, and faithfully teach it to the people. Finally, Sunday School leaders recognize that planning is essential to implementing its strategy.

Another Look at the Definition

 Return to the definition statement for Sunday School that you developed earlier. Compare it with the definition and the explanation you have just read. What are the differences? Does this new way of thinking about Sunday School have potential for your church's Sunday School ministry? What actions will you need to take to begin to communicate a new way of thinking about Sunday School? List some possibilities in the space that follows.

This book focuses attention on the Principle of Spiritual Transformation. That people may experience the divine work of spiritual transformation is to be the motivation for teaching. That is also our objective for teaching. That objective will influence the way lessons are taught, the methodologies employed, the curriculum materials that are selected, and the way space is used. Certainly it should influence the kind of people who are in Sunday School leadership roles including teachers. Therefore, as a general leader it is imperative you have a good understanding of transformational teaching for what it means to the direction and focus of your leadership. You will be a critical source for communicating the importance of this principle and its objective to those whom you lead.

Before determining some ways you can challenge your leaders to be transformational in their focus, examine in detail what spiritual transformation is, its relationship to Bible teaching, and some principles that influence its practice.

What Is Spiritual Transformation?

Reflect again on the definition of spiritual transformation.

Spiritual transformation is God's work of changing a believer into the likeness of Jesus by creating a new identity in Christ and by empowering a lifelong relationship of love, trust, and obedience to glorify God.

Here are some concepts that evolve from that definition.[4]

A Process

Spiritual transformation is a process—a progressive change of worldview, values, attitudes, and behavior. Beginning with the heart and reaching out to touch the life and witness of God's people at every level, God's Word and God's Spirit bring transformation. Spiritual transformation at its foundation is a change of the heart that expresses itself in the outward life.

God desires that believers be transformed into the likeness of Jesus. Knowing Jesus in an intimate personal relationship changes believers' hearts and transforms them into new persons. The most critical decision any person must make is to decide whether God is God. If He is, then that person's task is to know Him intimately and from that relationship to identify what God is doing and to join Him in it. The spiritual transformation of our lives comes through the renewing of our minds from thinking, seeing, feeling, and acting according to the pattern of the world to thinking, seeing, feeling, and acting like Jesus (Rom. 12:1-2; Eph. 4:12-16).

Paul expressed it this way to the Romans: "Don't become so well-adjusted to your culture that you fit into it without even thinking. Instead, fix your attention on God. You'll be changed from the inside out. Readily recognize what he wants from you, and quickly respond to it. Unlike the culture around you, always dragging you down to its level of immaturity, God brings the best out of you, develops well-formed maturity in you" (Rom. 12:2). This amazing transformation—from the inside out—is God's work. The change is not just outward appearance but a transformation of the essential person (one's character, nature, and perspective). It is more than a mere transition from one way of living one's life to a different way. It is becoming like Christ, to Whom the believer belongs and in Whom the believer dwells.

A New Identity

Spiritual transformation begins with a new identity in Christ. Salvation is a defining experience in which we become new persons. We take on His identity. Believers are sanctified or set apart for God's purposes at the moment of spiritual new birth in Christ (John 3: 5-6). At the moment of conversion God provides the new believer—

• *Justification.*—A believer is declared righteous on the basis of Jesus' death on the cross as He paid the full debt for every sin of a person's life (Acts 13:39). The record of sin is blotted out through forgiveness (Col. 2:13-15).

• *Regeneration.*—According to John 3:1-16, the regenerating work of the Spirit is to bring people to faith in Jesus, enabling them to enter the kingdom of God and have eternal life. The Spirit who brings people to a true knowledge of God through the gospel also will bring about practical expressions of that relationship with God in the lives of Jesus' followers.

• *Redemption.*—"Because of the sacrifice of the Messiah, his blood poured out on the altar of the Cross, we're a free people— free of penalties and punishments chalked up by our misdeeds. And not just barely free, either. *Abundantly* free!" (Eph. 1:7). The believer is set free from the guilt, the power, and the consequences of sin.

• *Deliverance.*—Believers are rescued from the domain of Satan, the power of darkness, and delivered into the kingdom of God. We enter into the present experience of eternal living conditions (Col. 1:13).

• *Sanctification.*—Believers are set apart to God's purposes because of the work of Christ and the operation of His Spirit in their lives. Disciples are separated from the world and from the Evil One (John 17:15-16), by being consecrated in the truth of God's Word (17:17). By this means they are liberated to bring blessing to the world as the agents of Christ (17:18).

A Growing Relationship

Spiritual transformation continues in a growing relationship of love, trust, and obedience. The analogy of spiritual birth suggests, as is the case with physical birth, that new believers are not born into full maturity in Christ. This does not mean a person is not eternally secure or is only partially redeemed in Christ. It does mean, as with any relationship, the depth and influence of our relationship with Him has the capacity to grow deeper and fuller. The Holy Spirit continues to help us develop the fullness of the new identity that we have in Christ.

Glorifies God

Spiritual transformation glorifies God. The goal of the new identity in Christ and the lifelong relationship of love, trust and obedience is to glorify God.

• God is glorified through a relationship of love. Love is to be the central characteristic of the believer just as love is the central characteristic of God.

• God is glorified by the believer's fulfillment of the mission of Christ (John 17:18; 20:21-23). The mission of Christ was fulfilled in making the love of God known. Our love for God, growing out of our trust in His Word, results in an inner spiritual likeness to Christ that reveals the person, love, grace, mercy, and power of God.

• God is glorified as He is made known to others through His relationship with His people: "This is to my Father's glory, that you bear much fruit, showing yourselves to be my disciples" (John 15:8, NIV).

Ways God Works to Transform a Believer into the Likeness of Jesus

Spiritual transformation begins and continues by the work of the Holy Spirit in the heart of the person who is saved by grace through faith (Eph 2:8-10). It is the work of the Holy Spirit (John 16:7-15). It is accomplished though our relationship with God in which we allow our inmost being to be transformed. Major agents of transformation are—

• *Scripture.*—The Word of God imparts His being to believers. His Word establishes us in a unique relationship with God with our obedience to Him set as an expectation. Jesus prayed, "Make them holy—consecrated—with the truth; Your word is consecrating truth" (John 17:17).

• *Family/home.*—God uses parents and other family members as His instruments of spiritual growth. "These commandments that I give you today are to be upon your hearts. Impress them on your children. Talk about them when you sit at home and when you walk along the road, when you lie down and when you get up" (Deut. 6:6-7, NIV).

• *The people of God.*—Jesus provides gifts to His church so that "we're all moving rhythmically and easily with each other, efficient and graceful in response to God's Son, fully mature adults, fully developed with and without, fully alive like

Christ" (Eph. 4:12-13). Every believer being transformed by the Holy Spirit is to help other believers grow in likeness to Christ.

• *Circumstances of life.*—God works in the situations of our lives. He can take the details or circumstances of the lives of those who love Him and shape them into something good (Rom. 8:28).

• *Spiritual exercises for godliness.*—Spiritual disciplines are the means by which we place ourselves before God for Him to work in us (examples: prayer, Bible study, fasting, worship, evangelism, serving, stewardship, learning). Even so, the most iron-willed discipline will not make us more holy since growth in holiness is a gift from God (John 17:17; 1 Thess. 5:23; Heb. 2:11).

• *God's discipline.*—God disciplines His children to make us holy and to transform us into the likeness of Christ (Heb. 12:10-11).

Evidence of Spiritual Transformation God Expects in a Believer's Life

The measure of discipleship is the degree to which a believer is like Jesus. What evidences mark a person as being like Jesus?

The believer is characterized by love, trust, and obedience. The believer has an awareness of loving God and being loved by God and remains in a relationship with Jesus, trusting in Him and living in His love. We do what He calls His own to do: to follow Him and to obey His commandment.

The believer lives in harmony with God's Word. The outward evidence of the inner spiritual transformation into the likeness of Christ is living by Jesus' teachings, His Word (John 8:31-32; 14:21,23,24), loving God and loving others (Matt. 22:37-39; John 13:34-35); and bearing fruit (John 15:8; Gal. 5:22-23). This focus on Scripture drives believers to discover biblical answers to life questions such as: What has God done? What is God doing in my life? Where is God going? How can God use my life? The believer strives to live out God's Word in all relationships such as husband-wife, parent-child, and church member-church family, as well as with the lost and in society in general.

The believer sees the world through the lens of Scripture. A believer is made different from the world by the Word of God (John 17:14). A biblical worldview provides a plumbline or frame of reference that drives how a believer thinks and acts (2 Tim. 3:16-17). As the Spirit transforms the mind, the believer is challenged to live by different values. "So if you're serious about living this new resurrection life with Christ, *act* like it. Pursue the things over which Christ presides. . . . See things from *His* perspective" (Col. 3:1-2). This will transform a believer's perspective on work in a secular society and on God-given opportunities to make a difference in the world.

The believer has a relationship with other believers. The Spirit brings believers together into a dedicated and distinct relationship with the Father, united as one spiritual family (the church), a people for His own possession and use. The Spirit of God dispenses spiritual gifts to believers to fulfill their purpose to do the work of ministry and build up the church (Rom. 12:4-8; 1 Cor. 12:12-31; Eph. 4:11-16).

The believer makes God's love known to others. A believer's love for God is reflected in loving people so much that the believer is compelled to make God known. The heart of the believer is focused on fulfilling God's purpose corporately and individually, to proclaim the good news of salvation by grace through faith in Christ that all people become believers. We are to go into our world and do the same thing Jesus was busy accomplishing. We are to make disciples who make disciples who make disciples . . . .

A clear difference exists between inner spiritual growth and outward activities that conform to a Christian way of doing things. Internal spiritual transformation—"Christ in you"—shapes the external life so that inward character and spiritual quality are evident in Christlike actions.

Activity-based transformation focuses on self, on things to do. These things may be good: prayer, Bible study, journaling, worship, witnessing, teaching, and ministering. But, there is a difference between inner spiritual growth based on love, trust, and obedience and simply participating in outward activities that conform to a Christian way of doing things. We must take care that we don't emphasize a rigor and intensity in this regard that gives the impression that the Christian life is more struggle than fulfillment or more depressing than hopeful. To live for Christ is to have victory over all things (1 John 5:4).

Has God Changed You?

Now evaluate yourself against the evidences of spiritual transformation God expects in the believer's life. Determine areas of strength and weakness. Where you determine yourself to be weak, make that area an item of prayer. Remember, we are not talking about ways you can make yourself better. This is a spiritual issue that requires a divine work. Make yourself available to God that He may continue His transforming work in your life. Each of us needs daily to experience the ongoing transforming power of the Holy Spirit within.

My life is characterized by love, trust, and obedience.

I am living my life in harmony with God's Word.

I see the world through the lens of Scripture.

I have God-honoring relationships with other believers.

I am dedicated to making God's love known to others.

These same evidences are to be seen in the lives of other Sunday School leaders and members who profess Christ and are being transformed by Him. As you consider the members of your Sunday School leadership team, do you sense they are people who are committed to being transformed? How can you encourage them at this point?

Some Challenges to Spiritual Transformation

Becoming a believer in Christ ensures a lifelong conflict. Jesus forewarned His disciples to that fact (John 15:18—16:4). Nevertheless, as believers we have been equipped for the struggle (Eph. 6:10-16).

Hindrances to transformation believers can anticipate include—

- *Satan.*—The struggle is real, but the victory is in Christ. Satan is powerless against Him. Jesus asserted, "The chief of this godless world is about to attack. But don't worry—he has nothing on me, no claim on me" (John 14:30). This powerlessness to defeat Christ is assurance to believers that we have that same power because we are in Christ.

- *The world.*—A believer faces temptation to conform to the world's perspective and its way of doing things. *World* in this usage represents everything that is totally opposed to God's love and purposes. The love of God cannot dwell in the same heart that loves the world. "Don't love the world's way. Don't love the world's goods. Love of the world squeezes out love for the Father" (1 John 2:15). "In this godless world you will continue to experience difficulties. But take heart! I've conquered the world" (John 16:33).

- *Personal desires (flesh).*—The old nature of self-centeredness engages the believer in a spiritual war against God-centeredness. Paul wrote a description apt to us all: "I truly delight in God's commands, but it's pretty obvious that not all of me joins in that delight. Parts of me covertly rebel, and just when I least expect it, they take charge" (Rom. 7:20). The situation is not hopeless, however. Paul continued: "I've tried everything and nothing helps. I'm at the end of my rope. Is there no one who can do anything for me? Isn't that the real question? The answer, thank God, is that Jesus Christ can and does. He acted to set things right in this life of contradictions where I want to serve God with all my heart and mind, but am pulled by the influence of sin to do something totally different" (Rom. 7:21-25).

• *Lack of faith.*—The person without faith is overwhelmed by what he faces. The Scriptures are filled with admonitions to live in faith. Jesus confronted His disciples as they struggled with His words about His pending departure. He said, "Don't let this throw you. You trust God, don't you? Trust me" (John 14:1). A few moments later Jesus challenged them to see the potential of faith. "Believe me: I am in my Father and my Father is in me. If you can't believe that, believe what you see—these works. The person who trusts me will not only do what I'm doing but even greater things" (John 14:12). John encouraged his readers with the assertion that "every God-begotten person conquers the world's ways. The conquering power that brings the world to its knees is our faith" (1 John 5:4).

• *Inadequate knowledge.*—The Bible is the source for understanding the way of salvation, understanding the gospel, and receiving guidance for daily living. To be deficient in studying the Bible is to set oneself up for failure and defeat. "Stick with what you learned and believed, sure of the integrity of your teachers . . . . There's nothing like the written Word of God for showing you the way to salvation through faith in Christ Jesus. Every part of Scripture is God-breathed and useful one way or another—showing us truth, exposing our rebellion, correcting our mistakes, training us to live God's way. Through the Word we are put together and shaped up for the tasks God has for us" (2 Tim. 3:14-17).

• *Unintentional drifting.*—Sometimes believers begin an unplanned drift and thus cease growing in Christ as they are supposed to do (2 Pet. 3:18).

• *Deliberate rebellion.*—Rebellion is saying no to God. Deliberate rebellion becomes a denial of love for God (John 14:24) and leads to spiritual stumbling (1 Pet 2:8).

• *Distraction.*—A believer can become distracted from the centrality of Christ to the peripherals of religion; from spiritual priorities to activities that may or may not be good things; from the victory we have in Christ to occupying our minds with our fears and failures; from the grace and mercy of Christ to the pursuit of legalistic self-righteousness; from God's purposes to personal ambitions; from a balanced relationship with Christ to preoccupation with one doctrine or aspect of the Christian life.

There is no substitute for living by faith in Jesus and growing in a relationship of love, trust, and obedience while yielding to the transforming power of the Holy Spirit. We can be encouraged to know that Jesus prayed for our protection (John 17:15) and through the Holy Spirit He is always available (John 14:16-18; Matt. 28:20).

What Challenges Do You Face?

Look again at the challenges to spiritual transformation. This examination is extremely personal, but which challenge or challenges offer you the greatest struggle? Once again, ask the Lord for His intervention. Pray to yield yourself more fully to Him that you may overcome that which impedes your effectiveness in living for Him and serving Him as a Sunday School leader.

The Biblical Basis for Teaching for Spiritual Transformation

The early church leaders gave themselves to the "ministry of the word" (Acts 6:4, NIV). The result was that the church grew in numbers and influence (Acts 6:7; 12:24; 19:20). What is it about the "ministry of the word" that leads to transformed lives and makes a difference in our effectiveness?

As we have affirmed, spiritual transformation is God's work of changing a believer into the likeness of Jesus by creating a new identity in Christ and by empowering a lifelong relationship of love, trust, and obedience to glorify God. What is the relationship between God's work of spiritual transformation and that of instructing people in God's Word, the Bible?

Spiritual Transformation:
Foundational to Biblical Instruction

Old Testament writers and prophets went beyond merely calling for God's Word to be "applied to life"; they insisted it be obeyed. In fact, the Hebrews believed that people could not truly know God's Word until they obeyed it (Ps. 119:32,34,128; Prov. 7:1-2). In the New Testament Jesus also stressed knowing and doing His teaching (John 8:31-32; 15:10,14; Luke 11:27-28). Perhaps no clearer or direct call for obedience to the Word is given than when James wrote: "Don't fool yourself into thinking that you are a listener when you are anything but, letting the Word go in one ear and out the other. Act on what you hear!" (Jas. 1:22).

As we identified earlier, Paul warned Christians not to conform to the world. *To conform* is to act in the same nature, character, perspective, and function in accordance with prevailing standards. The apostle urged believers to be transformed. To transform is to change the condition, form, character, or function of a person or thing. The transformation of which Paul speaks occurs by the continual "renewing of your mind" (Rom 12:2, NIV). *Mind* in this sense is broader than the seat of rationality. It certainly is that—a truth that should not be overlooked in favor of irrational emotion—but also includes knowing, feeling, and deciding. The word also implies the counsels and purposes of the mind.

Therefore, through the renewing of the mind the Holy Spirit transforms a person into the image and character of Christ, which is the goal of spiritual transformation. *Renewing the mind* describes the dynamic and mystical interaction of the Holy Spirit with the human spirit to control the mental processes—pushing out the old nature characterized by sin and replacing it with the new nature characterized by the fruit of the Spirit.

Together "mind" and "heart" encompass knowledge, thought, reason, and understanding—the whole of the conscious life. The believer begins by recognizing his or her position in Christ and then grows toward the moral and spiritual standard of Christlikeness. Both the position of being "in Christ" and the process of growth occur through a revolutionary metamorphosis as the Spirit of God permeates the center of thought, consciousness, and decisions. The Holy Spirit, the true Transformer in the biblical instruction process, transforms the unbeliever with a secular worldview into a believer with a Christian, biblical worldview.

"Worldview" refers to the collective set of fundamental convictions people hold and on which they base their actions. Worldview drives the way a person thinks and acts.

- Everyone has a worldview.
- Objective, independent reality exists apart from an individual's worldview. A person's perception of reality may be right, wrong, or a combination of both.
- A worldview is, by its nature, comprehensive; it filters all observations and covers all aspects of life.
- A person's worldview can change. Christians should desire to have their worldview transformed into a biblical worldview. A biblical worldview describes a worldview that is based on the Bible and reflects biblical convictions. It is, in fact, God's worldview or perspective on reality. It is thinking like God thinks.

God's Word—Indispensable to Spiritual Transformation

The first major agent of spiritual transformation is Scripture. Through God's Word, the Lord imparts His being to believers. "God means what he says. What he says goes. His powerful Word is sharp as a surgeon's scalpel, cutting through everything, whether doubt or defense, laying us open to listen and obey. Nothing and no one is impervious to God's Word. We can't get away from it— no matter what" (Heb. 4:12-13). When people place their faith in its message (Heb. 4:2), their hearts are cleansed (John 15:3). Such is the power of the Word of God—power to create faith in human hearts (Rom. 10:16-17), power to make clean (John 15:3), and power to sanctify (John 17:17).

The biblical model of transformation is prescriptive in that the Scriptures specify the standards that believers should follow and the call to be obedient and to grow in Christlikeness. As each person is transformed toward Christlikeness, the church is strengthened and with it, the culture of the community, the nation, and the world is transformed.

Throughout the Bible God reveals the place of His Word and His Spirit in spiritual transformation. Through the Scriptures God shows people who He is and who they are to be in relationship to Him. He has given people this revelation to study, assimilate, and obey through the life-changing power of the Holy Spirit. All knowledge of God comes through God's revelation of Himself to humankind. Thus both spiritual understanding and transformed lives have their source in God.

Instruction—What It Means to Teach People the Bible

Teaching and instructing people in the Word of God is essential to being a coworker with God (Col. 1:28; 3:16; 2 Tim. 2:2,15; 3:16-17). The result of such teaching is transformed lives—changed lives giving glory to God with obedience (Col. 3:7) and love that springs from a pure heart and a sincere faith (1 Tim. 1:5). Such Christlike love is the distinguishing mark that Jesus calls His disciples to demonstrate before a watching world (John 13:35).

God commands people to study His Word (Josh. 1:8; 2 Tim. 2:2,15) and to teach it to others (Deut. 6:6-9; Matt. 28:18-20). In the Old Testament, the Lord informed Moses that He would give him the Ten Commandments for the people's "instruction" (Ex. 24:12, NIV). In its most primitive form the Hebrew word for "instruction" means to throw or to shoot. Included here is a sense of direction. God's Word was not merely to inform minds but to direct people's lives. Moses gathered the people just for this reason (Ex. 35:1) and commanded all the people—men, women, children, and aliens—to assemble to listen and "learn to fear the Lord your God and follow carefully all the words of this law" (Deut. 31:12, NIV). Moses was especially concerned about the children who make up the next generation (Deut. 31:13).

In the New Testament, the Greek word for training as found in 2 Timothy 3:16 and Ephesians 6:4, *paideia*, means a blend of instruction, discipline, and personal guidance. Generally, *instruction* means to train or direct learners to build their lives upon a structure of authoritative precepts or truths. The instruction is best when characterized by a systematic plan and order and a call to conform to a rule or practice. Instruction also includes commands or directives (1 Tim. 1:5).

Instruction has an "edge" to it, in that those who instruct have a sense of urgency, passion, and seriousness about their task. Instructors typically deal with issues that change people's lives and warn of the consequences of failing to follow the directives. In the secular realm, flight instructors provide a good example. Flight instructors teach pilots with intensity not only because the life of the pilot is at stake, but also because the lives of passengers are on the line.

Instruction in spiritual matters also includes intensity and passion, for the eternal welfare of people is at stake. Bible teachers intentionally lead participants to the spiritual "fork in the road" that demands decision. Bible teachers are like "sign posts" directing travelers which way to go.

The concept of instruction reflects the heartbeat of the Bible (Ps. 32:8; 119:133; Prov. 16:20; Rom. 15:14; Eph. 6:4). Instruction is the mandate of the Great Commission (Matt. 28:19-20). Parents are responsible for instructing their children in the ways of God (Deut. 6:4-9; Eph. 6:4). The Bible is the source of instruction (2 Tim. 3:16). Ultimate direction to believers comes from God.

God directs His people to follow Jesus and to obey the teachings of Scripture through the power of the Holy Spirit in order to live out a biblical worldview. To live out a biblical worldview in a pluralistic, secular culture, every believer must understand the meaning and message of the Bible and what it means to live according to the rule of God in His kingdom.

Under the direction of the Holy Spirit, instruction for spiritual foundation and transformation includes—

• instruction by godly, loving parents who by word and example guide their children to integrate the Scriptures into the lives of their children influencing how they think and act;

• instruction by authentic Christian teachers who model the Christian way of life; and

• instruction of holy Scripture as the absolute authority and truth to guide all of life.

Instruction—Three Essential Elements

Look at these three areas more closely.

Biblical instruction in the home by parents.—Instruction through the home in partnership with the church is the primary biblical model by which the Holy Spirit transforms lives (Prov. 22:6; Eph. 6:4; 2 Tim. 1:5-7; Rom. 12:2).

In the early years, integrating biblical truth into life is primarily the responsibility of the family as parents nurture their children in partnership with the church. The Hebrew word for discipline includes both correction and instruction. In the Bible, especially the Old Testament, the largest number of teachers were in reality the parents.

In the New Testament, while the command in Ephesians 6:4 is specifically addressed to fathers, it can apply to either parent. Parents should be equipping their children to learn how to study and integrate God's Word into their own lives. As children mature, they become increasingly accountable for examining and integrating biblical truth into their own lives. Within the context of the home parents can teach an apologetic of the Christian worldview to their children, who are bombarded with many cultural worldviews. Anytime any parent learns a new truth from God's Word in worship, Sunday School, or personal Bible study, he or she should ask, "How can I help my child/children understand, live, and obey this truth I have just learned?"

Biblical instruction in the church by spiritually transformed teachers.—Biblical instruction in and through the church leads people to interact with God's Word in a ministry environment that is conducive to the Holy Spirit's work of spiritual transformation. Bible teaching is the continuous process and system by which believers, through instruction at home and among God's people, intentionally seek to convey the biblical worldview to others.

A biblical worldview includes the reality of God's grace as He has revealed the truth about who people are, how they fit in, and where they go when they die. The biblical worldview addresses a myriad of issues, including God's sovereignty and human sin, the absolute truth of Scripture, the necessity of a right and obedient relationship to God through salvation in Jesus Christ, the deliverance of people enslaved to sin and addictions, and the development of spiritual values and relationships through the transformational power of the Holy Spirit (Matt. 22:37-38).

Biblical instruction through the Scriptures themselves.—Bible study is the examination and integration of biblical truth into a person's life. While Bible study begins with understanding biblical content, Bible study should ultimately lead to spiritual transformation of individuals and groups. An individual can do such Bible study, but it also is to be done in fellowship with other believers and seeks to include unbelievers.

The Goal of Bible Study and Biblical Instruction: Transformed Lives

The goal of Bible study and biblical instruction is transformed lives that exhibit love for God and others (Matt. 22:37-40; 1 Tim. 1:5), that glorify God and are Christlike in nature (Ps. 119:1-16,105-112; 2 Cor. 3:18; Col. 3:16-17).

To achieve the ultimate purpose of Bible study and Bible teaching, participants must experience the Holy Spirit's ministry of sanctification. Sanctification is both a position and a process. "Positional sanctification" refers to who believers are in Christ— set apart at the moment of conversion (John 15:3; 1 Cor. 1:2). Sanctification as "process" refers to the ongoing lifelong ministry of the Holy Spirit in which He enables believers to "work out their salvation" (Phil. 2:12-13) through integrating biblical truth into the fabric of their hearts, thereby setting them apart from sin and equipping them for service (2 Tim. 3:16-17). Included in sanctification is the deliverance of people from demonic influence, addictive behaviors, and sinful attitudes.

Sanctification shapes persons' understandings of themselves, their world, and God. Sanctification conforms learners' worldviews to the biblical perspective. Sanctification occurs as the absolute truth and authority of God's Word become embedded in the minds of believers—from childhood to elderhood—through systematic Bible study, Bible reading, Scripture memory, and obedience to biblical teaching in all of life. Because of the changed worldview, attitudes, values, and behaviors are changed by the Holy Spirit to conform to the biblical model.

Is Your Sunday School Ministry's Purpose Being Accomplished?

You have written an initial statement that describes your understanding of Sunday School and its purpose. You also have considered the common understanding that others in your church have about the purpose of Sunday School ministry. And you have read the foundational premise that is influencing the message of this book as we consider a new way of thinking about Sunday School. You have seen what we mean by spiritual transformation and the relationship biblical instruction has to it.

Evaluating Your Perspective on Purpose

Now begin to evaluate or measure the effectiveness of your Sunday School in achieving its purpose. Respond to the following statements by rating them on a scale of 1 to 5 with 1 being low, 5 being high.

Our church has intentionally selected Sunday School as a seven-day-a-week plan for involving people in seeking the kingdom of God and fulfilling the Great Commission.

| 1 | 2 | 3 | 4 | 5 |

Our Sunday School provides a structure that enables the largest number of God's people to do the work assigned to the church: evangelism, discipleship, fellowship, ministry, worship.

| 1 | 2 | 3 | 4 | 5 |

Our Sunday School teachers and leaders are committed to engaging learners in the biblical model of instruction that leads to spiritual transformation.

| 1 | 2 | 3 | 4 | 5 |

Our Sunday School leaders and members are committed to building ongoing Bible study groups that are willing to reproduce themselves through birthing new groups at least every two years.

1   2   3   4   5

Our Sunday School leaders see themselves as more than teachers of facts and conduits of information but as models of the power and effectiveness of the gospel in the life of a believer.

1   2   3   4   5

Our Sunday School leaders and members are committed to discovering and enlisting the unchurched and unbelievers.

1   2   3   4   5

Our Sunday School leaders with children and preschoolers are committed to guiding preschoolers and children toward conversion through foundational teaching.

1   2   3   4   5

Our Sunday School leaders and members take deliberate steps to encourage unsaved people to come to faith in Christ.

1   2   3   4   5

Our Sunday School leaders and members are eager to assimilate new believers into the life of the church through involvement in small-group Bible study groups.

1   2   3   4   5

Our Sunday School leaders equip and support their class members in efforts to lead others to Christ.

1   2   3   4   5

Our Sunday School affirms the Bible as God's Word and as the textbook for understanding truth and for fully integrating truth into life.

1	2	3	4	5

Our Sunday School leaders accept the Great Commission as the mission mandate to God's people.

1	2	3	4	5

Our Sunday School leaders see Sunday School ministry as a way of fulfilling the mission of Christ for His church.

1	2	3	4	5

Our Sunday School leaders are committed to encouraging members to seek opportunities for service even if it means they must leave the class to do so.

1	2	3	4	5

Our Sunday School leaders affirm the Christian family as the primary institution for biblical instruction.

1	2	3	4	5

Our Sunday School leaders see themselves as servant-leaders whose objective is to lead people to faith in the Lord Jesus Christ and to build Great Commission Christians.

1	2	3	4	5

Our Sunday School leaders are willing to be held accountable for being faithful to their calling and assigned responsibility.

1	2	3	4	5

Our Sunday School leaders lead Bible study that facilitates the transforming work of the Holy Spirit in a person's life.

1	2	3	4	5

How did you rate? Did you find your Sunday School accomplishing its purpose? If not, pray that God would help your Sunday School fulfill its purpose. If you are accomplishing the purpose of Sunday School, ask God to expand that ministry.

Challenges to Your Purpose

Jesus faced challenges to His mission. Some were external; others were internal. Some came from expected sources, such as His opponents; others came from unexpected sources, such as His followers. Some challenges were to do things that were not bad in themselves but were not appropriate for achieving His mission.

The following questions deal with challenges to purpose. Identify the challenges, but don't stop there; no challenge is insurmountable in God's work (Phil. 4:19). Think about ways each challenge can be overcome. Commit yourself to praying about each challenge and develop a team of leaders and friends to join in praying for the Lord's guidance in overcoming the challenge.

As a general leader, what challenge hinders you from being the leader you have been called out to be?

What challenge does your church face in implementing Sunday School as its foundational strategy?

What traditions and practices exist that, under the microscope of purpose, do not help, and maybe even hinder, kingdom mission?

What challenge does your Sunday School ministry face in terms of discovering, enlisting, and training leaders?

What challenge does your Sunday School ministry face in terms of space, other physical resources, and financial support?

One Last Thought About Purpose

In *The Church on Purpose* Joe S. Ellis compared a swamp with a millrace as an illustration of the effect of purposefulness. He observed that a relatively small amount of water could set in motion a large waterwheel, which, in turn, could empower machinery to do its work. The key was in the narrow channeling of the water so that it struck the paddles of the wheel with force. On the other hand, a swamp might contain vastly more water but the water never accomplishes anything because it is not channeled in any precise direction. It is stagnate; hence, powerless and aimless. Ellis concludes that churches that are effective are more like the millrace. Ineffective churches are more like the swamp.[5]

Jesus knew what He was about. His purpose was clear. What about you? Your church? Your Sunday School ministry and its leaders? What are you about?

End Notes

[1] Frank Stagg, "Matthew," *Broadman Bible Commentary*, Volume 8, Clifton J. Allen, general editor (Nashville: Broadman Press, 1969), 97.

[2] Alvin J. Lindgren and Norman Shawchuck, *Management for Your Church* (Nashville: Abingdon, 1977), 46-47.

[3] Bill L. Taylor and Louis B. Hanks, *Sunday School for a New Century* (Nashville: LifeWay Press, 1999), 11.

[4] The material on Spiritual Transformation was adapted from "Spiritual Transformation: Growing More Like Christ," a paper developed by a team in the LifeWay Church Resources Division, LifeWay Christian Resources of the Southern Baptist Convention.

[5] Joe. S. Ellis, *The Church on Purpose: Keys to Effective Church Leadership* (Cincinnati: Standard Publishing, 1982), 24.

His Message Was Clear. What Are You Teaching?

Jesus' *message* was simple and clear: an announcement of the good news of redemption; a call for repentance; a challenge to live a radically different lifestyle in the kingdom of God. His message was a message of change—not the kind of change that comes from human effort; not the kind of change that comes from knowing more.

No, the change Jesus spoke about was a spiritual transformation. Through Jesus, one entered the kingdom and life was never the same.

The Message Jesus Came to Communicate

Jesus' call was certain. His purpose and approach were solidified. He also had an urgent message that needed to be communicated.

Throngs of people seemed to hang on every word as they crowded around Jesus to hear Him teach. A small group of men followed Him faithfully about the countryside. He taught them even more extensively the demands of kingdom life and what His disciples were expected to be. But His practice of teaching and the message He communicated were not limited to those groups or situations. In fact, He seized every opportunity to communicate the message to anyone He met.

Let's look at an instance in the life of Jesus when He engaged in one-on-one transformational teaching. The message He communicated in this encounter represents the message He came to communicate to the world. It is the message that is to be communicated clearly by all who teach for spiritual transformation.

His Message Was Clear

John the Baptizer had created no small stir in the rural region outside of Jerusalem. He was a strange-looking man in his camel-hair coat held in place by an authentic leather belt. His diet of wild honey and locusts also set him apart from most. Even more was the message he declared with a fervency unknown by his contemporaries: "Change your life. God's kingdom is here" (Matt. 3:2). If not in style at least in content, John sounded like the long-silent prophets of the past.

John was not self-centered, however. A critical aspect of his message, in fact, pointed away from himself to Another. Of this One, John declared, He "will ignite the kingdom life within you, a fire within you, the Holy Spirit within you, changing you from the inside out" (Matt. 3:11). Who was this One who would bring about such spiritual transformation? This change agent was Jesus.

Groups such as the Pharisees, who were deeply dedicated and committed to the practice of traditional religion, were both curious and offended by what John had to say. No doubt, the general public's interest in John heightened the Pharisees' interest in this unusual preacher—not that they were eager to embrace him or his message; rather, they felt threatened.

Their concerns were magnified by the appearance of Jesus of Nazareth, a dynamic new teacher. He too came preaching a message of the kingdom and issued a call for repentance. He obviously knew the Scriptures, for He used them frequently and effectively. He spoke with authority; yet, they knew He was not formally trained in the rabbinical school. He appeared to be a common man; yet, He acted with an unusual power that could only be attributed to a divine source. He declared a message that cut straight to the heart. His message was clear; hence, it could not be ignored.

One evening Nicodemus, a respected member of the powerful and influential Sanhedrin Court, arranged a visit with Jesus. Whether he came as a representative of that august body or as an interested individual is not clear. He may have accepted an assignment to investigate Jesus for the Sanhedrin because that would give him an opportunity to meet the Messenger, hear the message, and learn firsthand Jesus' views on the nature of the kingdom of God.

Nicodemus' interview with Jesus provided a memorable opportunity for Jesus to communicate His message. As John, the Gospel writer, recorded the story, he provided us what may be the most popular explanation of Jesus and His message found in Scripture.

A kingdom message.—Jesus went straight to the point in His teaching moment with Nicodemus. The issue was the kingdom of God. "Unless a person is born from above, it's not possible to see what I'm pointing to—to God's kingdom" (John 3:3). The kingdom of God had been His theme from the outset of His ministry. "He picked up where John left off: 'Change your life. God's kingdom is here' " (Matt. 4:17). Included was a call for repentance, a radical and deliberate turning to God that results in His work of transformation. Why change? Why repent? Because the kingdom of God was near.

Simply stated, the kingdom of God speaks of the rule or reign of God. It is not geographical or political in nature. "The kingdom of God is, first and foremost, relational. God wants to have a redemptive relationship with us. . . . He establishes and maintains that relationship through the saving grace of Jesus Christ."[1] The kingdom and kingdom work is God's work. People do not build it or maintain it. They enter it through repentance and faith in Jesus Christ. In that way they are opening their lives to be ruled by God.

In His preaching and teaching, Jesus extended an invitation to everyone to enter the kingdom. The kingdom is to be the priority (Matt. 6:33). Jesus taught His disciples to pray for God's rule—the kingdom—to be realized on earth just as His reign is realized in heaven (Matt. 6:10). While the kingdom is available in Christ now, the consummated kingdom or reign of God is futuristic. Only those who have submitted to the reign of God in Christ will be fit for the kingdom to come.

The reality of the spiritual dimension.—For many, reality is defined in terms of the five senses. If something cannot be touched, seen, heard, smelled, or tasted, then it is only theoretical and therefore suspect. Jesus came to challenge that notion. The spiritual dimension of life is real. It cannot be ignored. A person can only enter the kingdom of God when he releases himself from domination by the empirical and acknowledges the validity of the spiritual experience.

Nicodemus modeled the struggle of humankind at this point. He was a man of position, prestige, and power; a man of wisdom and wealth; a man with information, intelligence, and investment. He appeared to have it all. Yet his coming and inquiring of Jesus suggested dissatisfaction. Although Nicodemus was a religious man, he had difficulty thinking spiritually.

Look again at what Jesus said to him: "Unless a person is born from above, it's not possible to see what I am pointing to—to God's kingdom" (John 3:3). Nicodemus shows his lack of spiritual understanding when he responded by wondering how such a thing could be possible.

Jesus challenged Nicodemus by suggesting it is difficult enough to understand the things with which one is familiar, like the wind blowing. He might have said: If you cannot explain things with which you are familiar, like the wind blowing, how do you possibly think you can comprehend the deep things of God? The issue is not one of understanding, as if one is analyzing a process or sequencing an event. The issue is acknowledging the spiritual, submitting to God, and being willing for Him to do His spiritual work of transformation.

The way into the kingdom.—The essence of Jesus' discourse with Nicodemus is that kingdom life—the transformed life—is not something one does for self. It is what God has done for everyone who believes. The efficacy of God's transforming work in the life of a person is activated by that person's faith in who Jesus is.

Nicodemus began his conversation with Jesus in a courteous and complimentary fashion. He greeted Jesus as "Rabbi." This title, meaning teacher, was usually reserved for one who was formally trained. In addition, he acknowledged that Jesus was extraordinary: "We all know you're a teacher straight from God. No one could do all the God-pointing, God-revealing acts you do if God weren't in on it" (John 3:2). Yet, as commendable as this was, other teachers could have been given, and probably had, the same accolades.

Jesus was more than a profound teacher or a mind-boggling miracle worker. He was able to teach heavenly truth because He was from heaven—"I speak only of what I know by experience" (v. 11). He was able to do a divine work because He was divine.

With that in mind, Jesus proceeded to identify Himself with the Son of Man, His most oft-used self-designation with messianic implications. Perhaps He used this designation because it did not have the militant interpretations associated with the popular understanding of the Messiah.

Rooted in God's Word.—To further identify Himself, His purpose for coming, and the way to the kingdom, Jesus cited an Old Testament story with which Nicodemus would have been familiar (Num. 21). "In the same way that Moses lifted up the serpent in the desert so people could have something to see and then believe, it is necessary for the Son of Man to be lifted up—and everyone who looks up to him, trusting and expectant, will gain a real life, eternal life" (John 3:14-15).

Clearly, Jesus is the Son of Man who came to be lifted up for the sin of humankind. John summarized it this way: "This is how much God loved the world: He gave his Son, his one and only Son. And this is why: so that no one need be destroyed; by believing in him, anyone can have a whole and lasting life" (v. 16).

Many accept Jesus' humanity but not His divinity. Some may accept Him as teacher, but not as redeemer; as miracle-worker, but not as Savior. However, if a person seeks to enter the kingdom of God, he or she must accept Jesus as the Christ of God who came into the world to free humankind from the devastation of sin and make eternal life—the transformed life—a reality.

A willful choice.—Nicodemus was challenged to realize the ineffectiveness of his own pure bloodline, the failure of his religious orthodoxy and orthopraxy, and the meaninglessness of his personal achievements. Entering the kingdom was a matter of his will, not that he could "will" it to happen just because he wanted. However, if, under the conviction of the Holy Spirit, he chose Jesus by faith, spiritual transformation would be the result.

The kingdom comes in Jesus. The transformed life begins and continues by submission to the way of Christ. There is no other way (John 14:6).

How did Nicodemus respond to the teaching of Jesus? Did he understand? More importantly, did he believe? John 7:51 tells us that Nicodemus came to the defense of Jesus before the Sanhedrin. Following Jesus' death, Nicodemus openly participated in His burial and provided enough spices to bury a king. But even if Nicodemus had not chosen Jesus and the kingdom, that does not alter the truthfulness of Jesus' message and His faithfulness as the messenger. He remained true to His call and His purpose. His message was clear.

He Spent Time with His Father

We already have noted that, for Jesus, doing the will and work of the Father was like food to the body (John 4:34). We also observed that those who heard Jesus teach distinguished His teaching, both in content and in authority, from what they were accustomed to hearing from the formally trained teachers (Mark 1:22,27). His devotion to His mission and the difference in His teaching can be attributed to the time He spent in isolation with His Father—(John 14:10,24)—for prayer, meditation, and reflection.

Perusing the Gospel stories will turn up example after example of Jesus' separating Himself from others and the strain and stress of life to spend time with the Father. Here are a few examples.

• Jesus was in the wilderness desert for a time of spiritual isolation when the tests came from the devil (Matt. 4:1-2). It is not unreasonable to think Jesus was equipped for the time of testing because He had spent time with the Father.

• Jesus rose early in the morning to pray and came away with another affirmation of His purpose for coming (Mark 1:35-38).

• Jesus had concluded a personal prayer time when one of His disciples asked Him to teach them to pray (Luke 11:1). This is another instance in which Jesus modeled what He taught.

• Jesus spent the night in prayer prior to calling out the twelve (Luke 6:12-13).

• Jesus prayed a prayer of blessing before feeding the thousands (Matt. 14:19).

• Jesus was isolated in prayer just before inquiring of His disciples about their understanding of who He was and giving for the first time His own prediction about His death in Jerusalem (Luke 9:18-22).

• Jesus was in prayer at the time of the transfiguration, an event that provided another affirmation of who He was (Luke 9:28).

• Jesus prayed for Peter to have a stalwart faith in the face of temptation (Luke 22:31-32).

• Jesus prayed for the Father's will to be accomplished even as His accusers were coming to arrest Him (Mark 14:32-42).

• Jesus prayed for forgiveness for His executors (Luke 23:34).

• Jesus prayed a prayer of trust in His Father even as He died (Luke 23:46).

Surely those hours with His Father were critical in shaping Jesus' life, strengthening His heart, sustaining His spirit, and sharpening His mind for fulfilling His purpose and delivering His message. Are you spending time with our Heavenly Father?

He Knew the Scriptures

Another key to Jesus' effectiveness in being able to communicate His message clearly was His familiarity with Scripture. His message was rooted in the Word of God. Obviously, the Bible of Jesus' day was comprised of the books we know as the Old Testament. Jesus' formal education and home training as a youngster would have centered around the Law, the Writings, and the Prophets. The Gospel writers carefully placed Jesus' birth, life, ministry, and death in the context of Scripture (For examples, see Matt. 1:22-23; 2:16-17; 13:15-21; 21:4; Luke 22:37; John 19:24,28).

Jesus' familiarity with the Scriptures are seen in His direct use of Scripture (Luke 4:17-19), frequent references to Old Testament personalities (Luke 17:32) and events (Matt. 24:37-39), several indirect references to Old Testament concepts (Matt. 5:5; see Ps. 37:11), and His skillful use of Old Testament teaching to support His message (Matt. 21:42-44).

If we are impressed with what Jesus knew about Scripture, we can be inspired by His ability and skill in using Scripture as a guide for life. Once again, Jesus models an important element for building a ministry of transformational teaching. Transformational teaching begins with leading others to know the truth but has as its end that learners accept the truth and are transformed by the power of the Holy Spirit.

Think About Your Sunday School Ministry

What is the objective of the teaching that is taking place in your Sunday School classes and departments: teaching for information or teaching for spiritual transformation? Can you recall specific examples of persons whose lives have been spiritually transformed because of the teaching and influence of Sunday School ministry? (Remember, Sunday School ministry is not confined to what happens in a Sunday morning meeting period.)

Make some brief notes about those examples in the space that follows. You may prefer not to record names.

Look for ways to share these examples as a way both to tell the purpose of Sunday School ministry and to encourage others in Sunday School leadership roles. These stories may be used (with permission) in church newsletters, testimonies in worship, examples in Sunday School leadership meetings, or as part of the Sunday School ministry report during a church business meeting.

Now dream a little. *What would your Sunday School ministry be like if all its leaders were focused on teaching for spiritual transformation? What if every leader were committed to and equipped to teach evangelistically?*

Don't exclude yourself. As a general leader, you are to model what you expect of others. List some key elements of your dream in the space that follows.

Do You Know What Kind of Teaching Is Taking Place?

Maybe you found the earlier exercises difficult because you don't know what kind of teaching is taking place in your Sunday School classes and departments. Many general leaders don't because they are so involved with administrative tasks they find it difficult to be involved in Bible study groups.

Without meaning to minimize the other things you do, reaffirm the purpose for your Sunday School. How do those things that take the greater part of your time help carry out that purpose? These other tasks may have value, but teaching the Bible for spiritual transformation must be primary. And if you are a general leader of the ministry with that assignment, it is imperative that you know what kind of teaching is taking place.

Wayne Poling, a Sunday School ministry consultant at LifeWay Christian Resources, is committed to strengthening Bible teaching through Sunday School and helping general leaders in their ministry. He has suggested actions general leaders can take to increase their own awareness of the teaching that is being done.[2]

Review the list that follows. Place an *X* beside those actions that you are satisfied are done well. (We all can improve, but overall you are pleased.) Mark a *0* beside those actions that need attention. Highlight those actions that you will begin immediately to address.

_____ *Get to know the leadership team members.* They are your partners in ministry—team members in carrying out the strategy. Learn their names, know about their families, and interact with them. Everyone wants to be known as an individual.

_____ *Pray for the leadership team.* In praying together you will grow closer in the Holy Spirit and more unified as, together, you seek God's direction.

____ *Engage them in conversation.* This may be formal or informal, planned or spontaneous. Your goal is to learn how each person views his or her role, especially in relationship to teaching (We will see later that everyone is related to teaching even if their particular position is not as a "teacher.") Is teaching a means of presenting information or directed intentionally toward spiritual transformation? Search out examples of what the leader sees taking place in the lives of class members because of the teaching and ministry through the Bible study group. What kind of changes would the person like to see take place?

____ *Arrive early on Sunday morning to observe what takes places before and as members arrive.* Do leaders arrive early? What preparations do they make for teaching? Are the facilities, equipment, and supplies arranged for teaching? Is what is in place appropriate for the age group to be taught? How are members and prospects greeted and engaged by the leaders?

____ *Observe how leaders use the Bible teaching curriculum materials.* Are they using the resources the church has approved and provided? Do they know how to use the resources in ways that maximize the teaching time?

____ *Assess the general attitude of leaders you meet.* Do they appear eager and confident? Do you sense they know what they want to accomplish?

_____ *Observe how learners are engaged in the Bible study.* Are the approaches appropriate for the age group? Do you see variety in methodology?

_____ *Assess whether the leaders relate to members beyond the group meeting time.* Do they see members in their homes, contact them via telephone or email, or seize other serendipitous opportunities to relate to them?

Taking these actions will require you to learn about the kind of teaching that should be taking place in classes and departments. For example, to assess effective preschool teaching you will need to know some basics of teaching preschoolers. The age-group books in the *Teaching for Spiritual Transformation* series produced by LifeWay Church Resources are excellent resources to help.[3]

These actions also will call for you to "lead by walking around" rather than by "lingering around the Sunday School office." The results can be worth the change in your style or schedule.

Some Guidelines for Teaching for Spiritual Transformation

While some of the guidelines may seem self-evident, they are important and need to be followed by those who teach to see God change lives.

Use the Bible

The Bible reveals God's nature, His expectations of people, His plan for redeeming people, and His instructions for living according to His plan. Thus, the Bible is the authoritative guide for all of life and the textbook for spiritual transformation. The Bible leads people to know God, both intellectually and experientially. The historical accounts show God's involvement and intervention in the lives of persons. The ethical teachings show how people are to live in relationship to God and others. The eschatological portions of Scripture show their future in Him. Scripture points to the power, majesty, and work of God; and the proper human response to that revelation is to love, trust, and obey Him (2 Tim. 3:16; Heb. 4:12). No other religious studies, no matter how seemingly contemporary or relevant, are empowered by God's promise that His Word "will not return to me empty, but will accomplish what I desire" (Isa. 55:11, NIV).

Teachers and leaders also must learn to use the Bible properly (2 Tim. 2:15), as well as to encourage learners to use it as their primary source of instruction and teaching. Paul gave testimony that neither he nor those who taught with him did "distort" (NIV) or "adulterate" (NASB) God's Word (2 Cor. 4:2). How important it is for teachers to practice sound biblical principles of interpretation.

Depend on the Holy Spirit

The Holy Spirit is at work in God's world convicting people of sin and drawing them to God (John 16:8-11). The Holy Spirit is present in believers, revealing spiritual truth and enabling them to understand this truth, discern its application to their lives, and become transformed people. The spiritual transformation of lives occurs only through the Spirit's power.

The Holy Spirit is active and essential in spiritual transformation as the Teacher, Guide, and Empowering Agent. While selected facets of secular educational theories are useful in Christian education, following those alone will not achieve spiritual transformation. Bible teaching for spiritual transformation begins with teachers who pray and depend on the ministry of the Holy Spirit.

Teach God's Word in and Through the Family

The home is the first place where Bible teaching for spiritual transformation should occur.

The Law of the Old Testament called for parents to instruct their children in, through, and around the home (Deut. 6:6-8). The Proverbs called on children to listen to both the father and mother as they instructed them (Prov. 1:8-9). One of the best-known proverbs, 3:5-6, is actually an instruction from a father to his son.

In the New Testament, family relationships and responsibilities are addressed specifically. Paul's Letter to the Ephesians clearly states the principles that fathers are to take the lead in bringing up their children "in the training and instruction of the Lord" (6:4, NIV). A significant passage for the role of husbands and wives is 1 Peter 3:1-7. Peter's instructions first to wives and second to husbands are built on the assumption that the husband and wife spend time together in prayer (v. 7).

Because the Bible emphasizes the primary responsibility of parents and families in religious instruction, Bible teaching sessions and the resources used before, during, and after the sessions should support and encourage spiritual growth and understanding within the context of the home.

Magnify Relationships with Learners Wherever You Gather Them
The church is commissioned by Jesus Christ and empowered by the Spirit to teach people to know and understand God's Word and to challenge them to obey it and integrate it into their lives. Spiritual transformation through Bible teaching will occur within the fellowship of the church as people interact with each other in the presence of the Holy Spirit in groups conducive to facilitating relationships.

Because the ministry of teaching God's Word has power to transform lives from spiritual lostness to spiritual life, teaching God's Word in other places, including apartment complexes, office settings, campus equal-access clubs, or wherever people can be gathered, becomes a powerful strategy to fulfill the Great Commission (Matt. 28:18-20).

The principle is clear: Teaching people God's Word bears fruit when the instructor relates to the people in language, terminology, and concern enough to be creative. Teachers who instruct others in such a way that God transforms lives must connect not only to the learner's head but also to the learner's heart.

Hold Teachers and Other Leaders Accountable

Hold teachers and other leaders accountable for these actions.

To model spiritual transformation.—Spiritual transformation of Bible study group participants begins with the personal spiritual transformation of the teacher. Every teacher is also a learner. The teacher is to follow the example of Jesus, who modeled all He wanted to communicate. Jesus said, "I've laid down a pattern for you. What I've done, you do" (John 13:15).

Bible teaching moves beyond words; teachers are to live what they teach. Teachers will communicate more by their lifestyle than by their words. Jesus cautioned His disciples that "a student is not above his teacher; but everyone who is fully trained will be like his teacher" (Luke 6:40, NIV). Paul recognized the principle that learners imitate their teachers and employed it as a principle for teaching (1 Cor. 11:1; 1 Thess. 1:6-7; Phil. 4:8-9).

To teach people God's Word.—In the Great Commission, Jesus commissioned all believers to teach others to obey all that He said. Although the Holy Spirit gives special teaching gifts to some individuals within a church, any believer can be called to teach. The teacher is to teach for change. The role of the teacher is to create an environment and guide learning in ways that will facilitate the work of the Holy Spirit and will encourage the learners to be spiritually transformed (Matt. 28:19-20; Acts 15:35; Eph. 4:11-13; Col. 3:16; 2 Tim. 2:2; Jas. 3:1). This includes recognizing the ways in which learners learn best and their level of learning (1 Cor. 3:1-2; Heb. 5:11-14; John 16:12).

To build people.—Teachers are leaders. Every leader is responsible for living as an authentic witness of Jesus Christ. As a leader, the teacher is accountable for building people by strengthening relationships with and among the group, leading the lost to Christ, seeing that people are cared for, and developing new leaders for service through the ministries of the church.

Consider a group study of *Jesus by Heart,* by Roy Edgemon and Barry Sneed, to help leaders as they build a ministry of transformational teaching.

Lead Learners to Be Accountable

Just as teachers and leaders need to be held accountable, learners need to be held accountable.

For their spiritual transformation.—Preschoolers, children, youth, and adults learn in different ways and on different levels. The learner should accept a growing responsibility for learning and living as a faithful follower of Christ (1 Pet. 1:5-11). Individuals are responsible for allowing the Holy Spirit day-by-day to transform them to become more like Jesus Christ. Members need to view the Bible as the primary resource in transformation. The role of the learner is to study God's Word with a teachable heart and to obey the Holy Spirit's leadership (Rom. 6; 12:1-2; Eph. 4:20-24; 5:8-10; Phil. 3:7-14; Col. 1:9-12; 1 Pet. 1:13-16).

For sharing their lives with others.—Learners can teach other learners, especially by telling their stories of how God is working in their lives (1 Thess. 2:8). Every believer is important for the effective work of the church and is responsible for involvement in evangelism, discipleship, fellowship, ministry, and worship.

Engage in Evaluation and Reflection

Because of their strategic roles of influence, "Teachers are held to the strictest standards" (Jas. 3:1). Teachers are accountable for examining themselves and their faith. Teachers are accountable to their learners and should seek to understand the learning styles and the spiritual transformation of their learners. Teachers should evaluate how well they achieve teaching objectives of specific lessons, but especially spiritual transformation goals of leading people to faith in Christ and guiding them to grow in Christlikeness.

Improving Teaching in Your Sunday School Ministry

In a sense as a general leader you are a "teacher of teachers." Whoever enlisted you may not have described your role that way. In fact, this concept may be new to you. So, what can you do to help improve the teaching that takes place in the classes and departments in your Sunday School ministry? In conferences Poling has offered several suggestions that may be of help.[4]

- *Pray for your teachers by name.* Teaching for spiritual transformation is a spiritual work that calls for spiritual empowerment. You can do nothing more important than to pray for your Sunday School teachers.

- *Build congregational awareness of the life-changing purpose of Sunday School ministry and the importance of Bible teaching for spiritual transformation.* By sharing examples with them, their own understanding and expectations will grow.

- *Lead teachers to expect results from their teaching.* Some may need to be challenged; others may need to be encouraged. As a general leader, you will know the difference when you get to know leaders individually.

- *Provide leaders what they need to teach effectively.* This includes curriculum equipment, furnishings, other teaching aids, and so forth. Not every church can provide the ideal, but at the very least it can commit itself to provide the best it possibly can.

- *Train leaders.* This includes helping them know the age group they teach and appropriate approaches for teaching. It also includes knowing how to use the resources, how to prepare for teaching, how to teach, how to study and understand the Bible, how to witness, and more.

• *Conduct regular Sunday School leadership meetings.* If Sunday School is foundational strategy, then regular meetings of those who are to lead the strategy is essential, not optional.

• *Point leaders to other developmental opportunities.* Some may be self-study aimed at personal improvement and enrichment, others may be conducted as local church events, and still others can be offered by the local association or state convention. National leadership-development events are conducted at LifeWay Conference Center at Glorieta®, LifeWay Conference Center at Ridgecrest®, or in other regional locations.

• *Set high standards.* These standards and expectations are to be communicated as part of the enlistment process. See pages 31-32.

• *Help leaders get off to a good start.* Starting poorly can be discouraging. Do what needs to be done to help leaders begin well and form good habits.

• *Help leaders develop a plan for personal devotions that includes Bible study and prayer.* Introduce them to devotional resources. Suggest ways they can begin and maintain the practice of spending time with the Lord.

• *Encourage Bible study that exceeds the preparation time for teaching.* While most Bible teachers acknowledge they benefit personally from preparing to teach, encourage leaders to develop an approach for personal Bible study that continues their own spiritual transformation.

• *Recognize and encourage leaders.* This may be done corporately through an appreciation banquet but will be even more effective when done personally in conversation or through a brief note.

A Plan for Teaching That Transforms

Sunday School for a New Century curriculum resources produced by LifeWay Christian Resources are designed to facilitate teaching for spiritual transformation.[5] Teaching-learning centers around three major concepts: *Prepare, Encounter,* and *Continue.* Leaders prepare not only a lesson but also themselves. During the session leaders and learners encounter God's Word in the context of a Bible study group as, together, they acknowledge the authority of their lives; search the biblical truth; discover the truth; and personalize that truth. They struggle with the truth and decide whether to believe and obey it as they continue to live and learn in daily relationships, especially with their families. Ideally, participants experience all of these elements before, during, and/or after every session.

Critical to this teaching strategy are "open" Bible study groups for teaching both believers and unbelievers. Sunday School leaders must not assume that all participants have prepared for the session. Instead, the Bible teaching leaders are to introduce participants to biblical truth that can transform their lives both during and after the session. Leaders help participants to continue focusing on the truth after the session by using learner guides and devotional resources and by emphasizing personal and family relationships. During the next week's Bible study session, participants will have an opportunity to reinforce the truth.

Read on for details on how *Prepare, Encounter,* and *Continue* work in practice.

Before the Session: *Prepare* (2 Tim. 2:15)

The apostle Paul urged Timothy to develop "reliable leaders who are competent to teach others" (2 Tim. 2:2). Reliable leaders don't just happen; they are people of commitment, diligence, concentration, determination, integrity, spiritual maturity, gentleness, patience, and godliness (2 Tim. 2).

Furthermore, "reliable leaders" not only teach a lesson, they also *are* the lesson. They model what it means to live for Christ. Paul urged Timothy to "teach believers with your life: by word, by demeanor, by love, by faith, by integrity" (1 Tim. 4:12). He was confident enough to say to the Philippians, "Put into practice what you learned from me, what you heard and saw and realized" (4:9). The principle is bold, but true: People will remember the character of the leader more than the content of the lesson. How can a leader have that kind of spiritual confidence? It comes through preparation in two proven ways.

1. *Through the Leadership Meeting.*—Sunday School leaders gather together regularly to pray, to focus on the mission of Sunday School ministry and the church, to focus on relationships with coworkers and class members, and to give attention to Bible study. Together leaders gain ideas on how to prepare a ministry environment that engages learners in a study of God's Word. *Ministry environment* includes more than room setup; it also includes caring relationships that generate openness and participation. This meeting also is a good time to plan ways Bible study can continue in daily life, at home and in other settings.

2. *Through Personal Bible Study.*—Individually leaders prepare for God to use them to teach His Word and for learners to encounter God's Word. Effective leaders depend on the Holy Spirit, knowing He already is at work in the lives of participants. They focus on relationships; minister to individual needs; prepare to teach people God's Word in and through their family; and develop a lesson plan reflecting a variety of teaching-learning approaches including relational, musical, natural, physical, reflective, visual, and verbal. (For details on each approach, see pp. 134-138, Appendix C, and age-group books in this series.)

The teaching-learning process for transformation features seven Bible teaching elements common to all ages. As leaders plan for the session, they should reflect on how God is changing them and others into the likeness of Jesus by asking certain questions. The seven elements/accompanying questions also find expression in a good teaching plan for use during and after the Bible study session.

BIBLE TEACHING ELEMENT	QUESTION
Acknowledge Authority	Who or what is the authority that is in *control* of my life?
Search the Truth	What historical setting and key words are reflected in the *content* of this Bible text?
Discover the Truth	What eternal *concept* is the Holy Spirit revealing to me from this Scripture?
Personalize the Truth	In my life *context,* what is God teaching me personally from this Scripture?
Struggle with the Truth	What *conflict* or crisis of belief is the Holy Spirit bringing about in my heart and life?
Believe the Truth	What new biblical *conviction* is God leading me to integrate into my life?
Obey the Truth	How is the Holy Spirit changing my *conduct* in how I think, what I value, and the way I live?

The chart on page 100 shows interrelationships between Bible teaching elements and *Prepare, Encounter,* and *Continue.*

During the Session: *Encounter* (2 Tim. 3:16-17)

During the session leaders strive to bring participants into an encounter with the Lord as, together, they encounter His Word. Why the Bible? "There's nothing like the written Word of God for showing you the way to salvation through faith in Christ Jesus. Every part of Scripture is God-breathed and useful one way or another—showing us truth, exposing our rebellion, correcting our mistakes, training us to live God's way. Through the Word we are put together and shaped up for the tasks God has for us" (2 Tim. 3:16-17). Why would anyone want to study anything else?

When participants experience all seven teaching elements before, during, and/or after each Bible study session, they are placed in a better position to experience transformation by the Holy Spirit. Some learners may experience these elements as sequenced steps. Others may experience them in a different sequence or in repetition throughout a session or unit. Spiritual transformation may occur over a period of time ranging from several lessons to a lifetime. This is especially so when foundations are laid in younger years for spiritual conversion and transformation.

Every good Bible study session will have a flow to it. From the moment people arrive, activities must grab people's attention. Every participant comes to a Bible teaching session with an authority—recognized or unrecognized—that controls his or her life. Therefore, the beginning of the teaching plan attempts to focus every individual's heart toward learning biblical truth that connects with his or her life, or where he or she is "coming from."

Usually, the next part of the teaching plan engages people in searching the Scriptures for biblical content and concepts they can understand for their lives ("Search the Truth" and "Discover the Truth"). The content and concepts are personalized in the context of the participants' lives ("Personalize the Truth"). Inevitably, people will experience inner conflict as biblical truth intersects and confronts their lives ("Struggle with the Truth"). This conflict is resolved when biblical convictions are integrated into life by

Prepare　　Encounter　Continue

The ministry environment

God's Word in a Bible
study group

Teaching-learning in daily
living and relationship

*Sunday School
Leadership Meeting*

*Personal Bible
Study*

3 Essentials of Bible Teaching for Spiritual Transformation

Acknowledge Authority
(control)

Search the Truth
(content)

Spiritual transformation is God's work of changing a believer into the likeness of Jesus by creating a new identity in Christ and by empowering a lifelong relationship of love, trust, and obedience to glorify God.

Discover the Truth
(concept)

Personalize the Truth
(context)

Struggle with the Truth
(conflict)

Believe the Truth
(conviction)

Obey the Truth
(conduct)

change of belief, attitude, and action as reflected in the person's conduct and in a lifestyle of love, trust, and obedience that glorifies God ("Believe the Truth" and "Obey the Truth"). These principles are the basis of curriculum development for Sunday School for a New Century Bible study resources for all ages.

Leaders and members should come to the session prepared to meet people as well as the Lord. When they see someone they do not know, they should introduce themselves, say how glad they are the person has come, and learn about the person/family and activities. The ministry environment includes helping people feel important—just as Jesus acknowledged each person's value to Him.

After the Session: *Continue* (Col. 2:6-7)

If indeed it is strategy, Sunday School will be more than an organization or a program that meets at a particular time. Teaching will not stop when the session is over. Teachers will continue their teaching ministry no matter the time, place, or situation. Consider these and other tips to help teachers develop a "24-7" ministry:

- *Practice* a daily quiet time of reading the Bible.
- *Pray* for the people and families in your class, by name.
- *Contact* at least one person on roll each week. Involve yourself with learners by calling or emailing them at home, school, work, or other convenient setting. If present for Bible study, ask: "How has our last Bible study helped you and your family this week?" To absentees, explain what was studied. With all, try to find out more about them and their family situation and ways Sunday School can be more supportive to their spiritual growth.
- *Visit, call, write, or otherwise contact prospects.* Take prospects a learner guide and/or devotional guide. Offer to explain the plan of salvation or other features related to that week's Bible study.
- *Help plan* fellowship or ministry events.

They become examples of the Christlike life who daily spend time with the Lord, pray for their group members/families by name, make constant efforts to stay in touch with members and prospects, build fellowship, and engage in ministry. They continue teaching by enlisting class or department members who become participants in teaching. They continue teaching by modeling the abundant life. As Paul exhorted the Colossians, "Now do what you've been taught. School's out; quit studying the subject and start *living* it!" (Col. 2:6-7).

Effective Sunday School leaders hold themselves, as well as their learners, accountable for obeying what God's Word teaches from Sunday to Sunday. Every Bible study participant expects the teacher to come prepared to teach, and rightfully so.

What if *participants* came prepared to report on what God taught them or how God had used them in ministry since the previous Bible study session? What if they brought someone who needed to hear God's Word? That indeed would be teaching that transforms lives.

End Notes

[1] Gene Mims, *Kingdom Principles of Church Growth* (Nashville: Convention Press, 1994), 12.

[2] Adapted from Wayne A. Poling, "Help Teachers Catch the Vision," *The Sunday School Leader,* March 2000, Vol. 5, No. 7, 15-17.

[3] For information about this series or to place an order, call Customer Service Center, 1-800-458-2772. Also visit these Web sites: *www.lifeway.com* or *www.lifewaysundayschool.com.*

[4] Poling, *The Sunday School Leader.*

[5] To secure a catalog of Bible study curriculum resources available from LifeWay Church Resources, call 1-800-458-2772. Also visit these Web sites: *www. lifeway.com* and *www.lifewaysundayschool.com.*

He Invested Himself in Others. What Kind of Investment Are You Making?

Jesus invested Himself in others. He "connected," in the *marketplace* of His daily life, with many different kinds of people—people of questionable reputation; people whom others did not like; people who seemed to have nothing to offer in return. He spent time with them, listened to them, responded to their needs and hurts. He seized every opportunity and moment to touch a life. Many responded to Him in faith and were spiritually transformed. Even that was not the end. Some of those same people became agents of spiritual transformation themselves.

Jesus Invested Himself in Others

In contemporary circles we may assess leaders as either task-oriented or people-oriented. Most leaders are weighted one way or the other. The ideal for which we strive is to be leaders who are balanced between a focus on the task we are to accomplish and a focus on the people with whom we relate.

If anyone ever had leadership style in balance, it was Jesus. We have seen how He clearly understood and gave attention to His purpose—His task—for coming to this world. But Jesus also was the ultimate people person. He must be so, for His reason for coming and people could not be separated.

As John declared, "He came to his own people. . . . The Word became flesh and blood and moved into the neighborhood" (John 1:11,14). Through one of His most well-known stories, He taught what is meant to be a good neighbor (Luke 10:29-37). Furthermore, He demonstrated it in the way He related to others.

Jesus and Crowds

Jesus lived in a crowded world. It may not have been as crowded as our world, but still, relatively speaking, His world was a crowded place. The Gospels describe several situations where crowds of people were around Jesus as He moved through the cities and villages. Even out in the rural landscapes people thronged around Him. These crowds were not always orderly and quiet; sometimes they were noisy and disorganized. People pressed upon Him to hear a word, feel His touch, or make a request of Him.

For us crowds may generate various emotions or reactions: fear of an angry mob raging on a street corner, anger at the mass of people who slow or prohibit our movement through the shopping mall; curiosity at seeing a group of people spontaneously gather in a public area; excitement by a crowd cheering in support of a cause with which we agree. But Jesus offered a different perspective on viewing crowds.

"When he looked out over the crowds, his heart broke" (Matt. 9:36). Jesus saw people who were harassed or wounded, maybe not always in the flesh but in their spirits. He knew that the deepest wounds are not always those that bleed. The people Jesus saw were helpless, like a people who had been cast down, physically and emotionally, and left disabled by their adversaries. He saw people who were "confused and aimless . . . like sheep with no shepherd" (v. 36). They ran in all directions, because they had no one to direct them. No one cared about them.

 Do your own Scripture search. Use your imagination and walk through the Gospel stories with Jesus, especially in those situations where He is jostled or pressed by the crowds. Watch for yourself how He responds.

What lessons can we learn about the way Jesus viewed crowds?

Jesus Always Saw the Individual

We tend to see crowds as a sea of faces. When He looked at a crowd, Jesus had the remarkable ability to see the individuals who made up those crowds; to hear their cries of help—both the cry of the voice and the cry of the heart.

- In a crowd on the main street of Jericho, out of the many sounds that likely filled the air, He heard one particular voice, that of Bartimaeus, a blind beggar, crying out for mercy (Mark 10:46-52).

• While walking along the seashore with a crowd, He saw one particular face, that of Matthew Levi, a tax collector of Capernaum in whom Jesus saw potential (Matt. 9:9-13).

• While walking through the crowded pool area of Bethesda, where many came in hope of experiencing the relief of the therapeutic waters, He saw one particular ailing body, that of a paralyzed man who needed more than strong legs. He needed a changed perspective on life that comes from a transformed heart (John 5:1-15).

In each case and in many other similar ones in crowded conditions, He saw, He heard, He identified an individual in that crowd. In essence, when Jesus saw a crowd, He said to each person in that crowd, "Hey! I know you are there."

Jesus Always Saw Beneath the Surface

Jesus saw more than faces or the obvious external need. He looked behind those faces to see the pressures that were bearing down upon them—the real needs that existed in their lives.

• He looked beneath the paralysis of a man brought to Him by four friends and dealt with the problem of his sin (Mark 2:1-5).
• He looked beneath the anxiety of a centurion over the sickness of his servant to commend him for his faith (Luke 7:1-18).
• He looked beneath the wild actions of a Gerasene man to inquire about his name, an expression of His desire to know the man (Mark 5:1-9).
• He looked beneath the curiosity of a short, and exceedingly unpopular, tax collector to see his deep desire for acceptance (Luke 19:1-10).
• He looked beneath the reluctance of an unsavory Samaritan woman to see her need for a changed life (John 4:1-26).

Jesus knew there is more to a person than what can be seen on the outside. He probed deep within to encounter the person at the point of his or her real need, to discover the authentic person who was hidden beneath veneers that had been set in place as a means of coping with life.

Jesus Always Saw with Compassion

Whereas we may respond to crowds with anger, curiosity, fear, or excitement, Jesus responded with compassion. Compassion is much more than feeling pity or sympathy. Someone said, "Sympathy sees, and says 'I'm sorry.' Compassion feels, and whispers, 'I will help.'" The difference is the degree of involvement and identification with the person who suffers.

Jesus' compassion was genuine. Because it was, He could not possibly reject those who hurt, withdraw for His own convenience and comfort, or neglect His Father's appointed purpose. His divine compassion and commission compelled Him to do something.

Therefore, invariably He was moved to act. Even at the risk of personal criticism, Jesus went to where He was needed. He spoke a word of comfort and care. He extended His hand to deliver a powerful, healing touch. Eventually, He would give His life as the greatest demonstration of love the world has ever known.

Jesus and Individuals

As we have affirmed, Jesus related to people as individuals not just as components of a group. Look more closely at one encounter that represents how Jesus dealt with individuals.

He Gave of His Time

More often than not, working with an individual at the point of his or her need requires more involvement than dealing superficially with needs in a group setting. Typically, when Jesus identified an individual in a crowd, He took time for that person.

Jesus' encounter with Bartimaeus of Jericho, though it can appropriately be considered a divine appointment, was spontaneous in that it was not an intentional, structured encounter. Jesus was on His way with His disciples to Jerusalem for Passover. As He moved through the countryside and small villages the crowd of fellow pilgrims swelled.

Passing through the congested streets of Jericho, which lay only a few miles from the magnificent city of the temple, Jesus heard the plaintive cry of this blind beggar. The perceived insignificance of this man by most may be seen in that he is known only as Bartimaeus, which means "son of Timothy." That would be akin to saying about someone, "He is Timothy's boy," as if the boy had no name of his own or if he did, no one had taken the time to learn it. Maybe that is how some felt about this blind beggar, especially those who were accustomed to seeing him along the village streets.

Given the noisy conditions along the crowded street and the preoccupation the travellers had with reaching their destination, some may not have heard Bartimaeus cry out. Others may have heard him but chose to ignore him simply because they felt no obligation to respond. Yet others certainly did hear him but urged him to be quiet, perhaps embarrassed by his very presence. Jesus, on the other hand, heard him, stopped, and called for him.

German pastor-theologian Helmut Thielicke observed:

> Though the burden of the whole world lay heavy upon his shoulders, though Corinth and Ephesus and Athens, whole continents, with all their desperate needs, were dreadfully near to his heart, though suffering and sinning were going on in chamber, street corner, castle, and slums, seen only by the Son of God— though this immeasurable misery and wretchedness cried aloud for a physician, (Jesus) has time to stop and talk to the individual. He associates with publicans, lonely widows, and despised prostitutes; he moves among the outcasts of society, wrestling for the souls of individuals. He appears not to be bothered at all by the fact that these are not strategically important people, that they have no prominence, that they are not key figures, but only the unfortunate, lost children of the Father in heaven. He seems to ignore with a sovereign indifference the great so-called "world historical perspectives" of his mission when it comes to one insignificant, blind, and smelly beggar, this Mr. Nobody, who is nevertheless so dear to the heart of God and must be saved.[1]

In spite of the fact that Jesus was on His own journey, surrounded by His own circle of friends, and dealing with mounting pressure and opposition from religious leaders, He stopped upon hearing Bartimaeus' cry for mercy. It is significant that Jesus took time for the man and as a result the man became a follower (Mark 10:52).

He Gave a Life-Changing Word

Jesus had a word for those whom He encountered. In Section 3 we developed a summary of the message Jesus had come to share. We saw how the message was delivered in what may have been a planned encounter with Nicodemus. Jesus also delivered His message to crowds assembled on the mountainsides (Matt. 5:1), by the lakeshore (Luke 5:1), and on the plains (Luke 6:17) He even had a word for this outcast on the crowded streets of a small town.

The message to Bartimaeus began with inquiry: "What can I do for you?" (Mark 10:51, NIV). Jesus would not force Himself even on a blind beggar. The question provided Bartimaeus a moment to reflect on his need and in responding to invite Jesus to act in his life. "The blind man said, 'Rabbi, I want to see' " (v. 51, NIV) That was his immediate need, at least as Bartimaeus perceived it. Jesus replied, "Your faith has saved and healed you" (v. 52).

Jesus understood Bartimaeus' need at its deepest level. As is typical in an encounter with Jesus, Bartimaeus got more than he expected. Jesus met the immediate concern of his life—sight—and the deepest need of his life—salvation. Either way, this was a life-changing experience. Bartimaeus could now be described as "formerly blind." And while the story initially had Bartimaeus "sitting alongside the road" (v. 46), the account ends with the assertion that Bartimaeus "followed Jesus down the road" (v. 52).

We are left only to speculate on just what that phrase means and to imagine the difference Bartimaeus personally made in the lives of others as he described his own encounter with Jesus. We hear no more about him in the Scriptures. But other examples demonstrate that those who came to know Jesus in turn invested themselves in others by telling their story of Jesus. It is not unreasonable to believe Bartimaeus did the same.

Here are other examples:

• The shepherds who saw Jesus as a Babe in a feeding trough could not help but declare what they had learned about Him and praise God for their encounter with God's glory (Luke 2:17,20).

• Andrew could not resist finding his brother, Simon, to take him to the Messiah (John 1:41).

• The woman of Samaria eagerly returned to her own city and invited them to come meet Jesus (John 4:28-29).

• Matthew Levi threw a large dinner party at his house for his disreputable friends to met Jesus (Luke 5:29-32).

• Legion, the wild man of the Gerasenes, went throughout a 10-city region to tell how much Jesus had done for him (Mark 5:20).

The examples continue beyond the biblical record into the history of the church. Countless people who have come to know Jesus could not help but tell others about Him. Some are world-renowned, like William Carey, Adoniram Judson, Lottie Moon, Billy Graham. Others are lesser known, some virtually unknown, but they shared their story of Jesus with others—with us.

And now it is our time to tell the story. That is the strategy of Jesus: Go make disciples by telling and by teaching, so that those who hear and are taught will obediently enter the circle of service by becoming themselves those who tell and teach.

He Gave Himself

Jesus' response to others was a personal investment. Look again at His encounter with Bartimaeus. In response to Bartimaeus' persistent cry for mercy, "Jesus stopped in his tracks. 'Call him over.' " (Mark 10:49). Bartimaeus responded with immediacy. "Jesus said, 'What can *I* do for you?' " (v. 51, emphasis added). This was a personal offer on Jesus' part. He was willing to give of Himself. He did not ask one of the twelve or any of the citizens on the street to do anything for this man. Neither did He ask Bartimaeus what he wanted someone else to do for him.

Obviously only Jesus could meet the immediate and deepest need of this man's life. The point is, Jesus wanted to meet it. He made Himself available to Bartimaeus. He was willing to give Himself to this struggler who had likely been rejected by many most of the days of his life. Because He did invest Himself, He made a difference.

We are reminded once again that finally Jesus would give Himself completely. And by doing so, He made it possible for all who are blind in spirit to see, rejected by others to be accepted by God, and begging for mercy to lavish in the riches of divine love and grace.

What Kind of Investment Are You Making?

Sunday School ministry with a focus on teaching for spiritual transformation is targeted toward people. That stands in contrast to an organization or program of teaching that is aimed toward duplicating the organization or expanding the program. The goal is not even to grow the church. We are on a kingdom mission, telling the kingdom story, and leading people to be spiritually transformed that they may become participants in the kingdom both as citizens and servants, those with privilege as well as responsibility.

Keeping the people perspective by investing in and connecting to people is critical to the effectiveness of Sunday School as strategy and transformational teaching as a best practice. General leaders set the pace by their own conviction, practice, emphases, and standards for success.

Leading By Example

Use the statements below to evaluate your own investment practices—not those kinds of investment practices that you hope will result in financial gain, but the investments you are making in people, both coworkers and members and prospective members.

Select the evaluative phrase that best describes your relationship to each statement.

Love for God and for people is my primary motivation for reaching out to others (Matt. 22:37-40).

Very Descriptive   Somewhat Descriptive   Not Descriptive

I am overwhelmed with compassion by the very thought that masses of people in my community have not been reached for Christ (Matt. 9:36).

Very Descriptive   Somewhat Descriptive   Not Descriptive

I am drawn toward ministry to the sorrowing and suffering even when I don't know the people personally (Luke 7:12-13).

Very Descriptive   Somewhat Descriptive   Not Descriptive

My caring is expressed in and supported by my willingness to act on another person's behalf (Matt. 15:32-39).

Very Descriptive   Somewhat Descriptive   Not Descriptive

I am willing to reach out and touch even those whom others reject (Mark 1:40-41).

Very Descriptive   Somewhat Descriptive   Not Descriptive

I am committed to loving my coworkers in word and deed because I know a loving attitude is evidence of discipleship (John 13:34-35).

Very Descriptive   Somewhat Descriptive   Not Descriptive

I am committed to creating an atmosphere of acceptance in all the classes and departments of our Sunday School ministry (Mark 2:15-17).

Very Descriptive   Somewhat Descriptive   Not Descriptive

The effective leader—the kind of leader you want to be—will possess and demonstrate qualities, attitudes, and other attributes that speak of the love and compassion of Jesus Christ. If these qualities are in your heart, they will be caught by your coworkers. In turn, members of their classes and departments will build off that dynamic so that in time the Sunday School ministry of your church will be seen as one that eagerly and willingly invests itself in people.

Without meaning to discount the value of recording attendance and the objective of reaching as many people as possible through Sunday School, as a general leader your primary concern will move beyond "How many did we have today?" to "How were we able to make a difference in people's lives today?" In fact, when investing in the lives of others becomes a priority, the record-keeping process used in your Sunday School ministry will need to be designed to track that kind of progress in addition to the number in attendance.

 With that in mind, what are the kinds of disciplines or actions you would measure or record to help evaluate the investment the Sunday School ministry is making in people? List some in the space below.

Did you include things like—
- members' and leaders' participating in visitation;
- number of visits made;
- gospel presentations made;
- information on those who professed Christ;
- ministry actions taken;
- members' and leaders' participating in evangelistic and personal discipleship training and development events; and
- personal-worship, Bible-reading, and stewardship practices?

Building Leaders Who Invest Themselves in Others

We are committed to reaching people because that was Jesus' commitment. We also have been given the responsibility of caring for one another (Phil. 4:1-4; Gal. 6:1-2). Caring for others is evidence of a healthy church—one that is doing more than going through the motions of being church but is living out its commitment as a people of God. Obviously, good health is essential to growth in any living thing.

What are some qualities you can lead your Sunday School leadership team to acquire that contributes to effectiveness in ministry, expresses concern for others, and leads to improved church health? The presence of each of these qualities in the lives of the leaders becomes a reinforcement of what is taught in the Bible study sessions. In this respect, the leaders become the lesson.

Lose yourselves in others. This is not a call to ignore yourselves, but it is a challenge to look beyond yourselves to others and ways that you can lend them a helping hand.

Listen intently. This statement is founded on two assumptions. One, as leaders you are in situations where you can dialogue with people. It also assumes that as the leader you are not doing all the talking. Sometimes, listening needs to take place between the words actually being spoken and the true concern being expressed.

Love the unlovely and the unloveable. People are different. Most of us are more comfortable being with and talking to people who are more like us. We need the Lord to set us free to be leaders who accept others no matter their racial, cultural, social, financial, lifestyle, or educational differences.

Care for one another. This includes leaders caring for one another; leaders caring for members; members caring for leaders, other members, and others who are part of our communities; and so forth.

Lead others to Christ. Through Bible teaching, ministry, fellowship, and relationships, share the transforming gospel message of Jesus Christ. Equip leaders and members to be effective personal evangelists.

Making Intentional Plans to Invest in Others

At one time the church was the place society looked to for help in responding to human need. That no longer is the case. In a more secularized society the church has relinquished care to other entities. Hospitals take care of the ill. The government provides financial support. The mental health agencies provide counseling. The funeral home takes charge when death comes. Even in religious matters, para-church group meetings and telecasts by preachers and teachers, and the proliferation of religious Web sites offer challenges to the preaching and teaching efforts of the church.

Even so, we cannot continue to give away our responsibilities. The church is an assembly of the called charged to reach out to the world. Sunday School is the foundational strategy for doing so. The effectiveness of the strategy is in part dependent on the willingness of its leaders to invest themselves in others.

Here are some ideas through which Sunday School leaders can invest themselves in others. Circle those that are currently being implemented in your church's Sunday School ministry. What preparations need to be made to implement the others?

• Members and prospects are prayed for regularly by name.
• Members and prospects are visited by leaders.
• Leaders are trained in evangelism and ministry actions.
• A systematic plan is in place to contact absentees.
• Fellowship activities are planned that bring members and prospects together in situations that aid in relationship building.
• Classes and departments are organized so that enough leaders are available to respond to the needs of members and prospects.
• A plan is in place for assimilating new members into the class or department immediately.
• Class and department leaders make intentional plans to meet and greet members and prospects who attend the Bible study group.
• Weekly planning includes time for leaders to discuss the needs

of members and prospects and ways to address those needs.
- Leaders plan Bible study with members and prospects in mind.
- Leaders are more intent on responding to people than on presenting lessons.
- Curriculum conducive to creating and maintaining open Bible study groups is selected and used.
- A ministry of prayer is established where members are involved in praying for one another.

Through the FAITH Sunday School Evangelism Strategy® many of these investments in people are accomplished in an ongoing fashion. By combining Sunday School and evangelism, FAITH creates weekly opportunities to go into the marketplace and to effectively meet many people at their point of greatest need—to know Christ personally. At the same time, Sunday School ministry is done. The necessity of ongoing planning/communication, prayer, and assimilation becomes evident, strengthening many Sunday School ministries. Many FAITH churches report they would do FAITH even if no one ever made a profession of faith, simply because of what it does for their members—turn them into more confident, enthusiastic Great Commission Christians.[2]

Test the People Focus of Your Sunday School

Evaluate the extent to which each of the following phrases is descriptive of your church's Sunday School ministry.

1. Leaders have the "big picture" of Sunday School as a 24-7 foundational strategy for evangelism and discipleship.

Very Descriptive   Somewhat Descriptive   Not Descriptive

2. Leaders are committed to the concept of teaching for spiritual transformation.

Very Descriptive   Somewhat Descriptive   Not Descriptive

3. Leaders accept the concept that the "leader is the lesson."

Very Descriptive   Somewhat Descriptive   Not Descriptive

4. *Leaders have hearts of compassion and concern for others.*

Very Descriptive   Somewhat Descriptive   Not Descriptive

5. *Leaders carry out actions that demonstrate their compassion and concern.*

Very Descriptive   Somewhat Descriptive   Not Descriptive

6. *Leaders are committed to giving the time necessary to reach, teach, and disciples others.*

Very Descriptive   Somewhat Descriptive   Not Descriptive

7. *Leaders prepare to do their work.*

Very Descriptive   Somewhat Descriptive   Not Descriptive

8. *Members experience high quality Bible study that focuses on spiritual transformation.*

Very Descriptive   Somewhat Descriptive   Not Descriptive

9. *In Bible study members are taught how to relate to God and to others.*

Very Descriptive   Somewhat Descriptive   Not Descriptive

10. *Members feel they are part of a class that genuinely cares for them.*

Very Descriptive   Somewhat Descriptive   Not Descriptive

11. *Members know one another and genuinely are interested in one another.*

Very Descriptive   Somewhat Descriptive   Not Descriptive

12. *Members help one another in times of need.*

Very Descriptive   Somewhat Descriptive   Not Descriptive

13. *Members minister to people outside the class and church.*

Very Descriptive   Somewhat Descriptive   Not Descriptive

14. *Members know how and regularly share their faith with others.*

Very Descriptive   Somewhat Descriptive   Not Descriptive

15. *Members make newcomers feel welcome and accepted.*

Very Descriptive   Somewhat Descriptive   Not Descriptive

16. *Leaders select and use curriculum that facilitates open Bible study groups that reach new people during any session.*

Very Descriptive   Somewhat Descriptive   Not Descriptive

17. *The pastor and other key leaders prayerfully consider using FAITH as the church's intentional plan.*

Very Descriptive   Somewhat Descriptive   Not Descriptive

It's All About Change

We have affirmed that Jesus came to encounter and connect with people and bring them into a right relationship with God. To do so, He invested Himself in them. He penetrated their lives and as a result they were spiritually transformed. As Paul expressed it, "Anyone united with the Messiah gets a fresh start, is created new" (2 Cor. 5:17).

We are called to be messengers of transformation, to penetrate our world, everyone we encounter, with the truth that makes a difference. Jesus used several figures to describe what He expects His people to be and do and what His own work was about. We are to be salt and light. He has given us the keys to the kingdom. Jesus compared Himself to bread and water. He said His kingdom was like leaven.

Elton Trueblood offers an interesting insight into the figures Jesus used. He notes that each represents some kind of penetration that brings about change.

> The purpose of the salt is to penetrate the meat and thus preserve it; the function of light is to penetrate the darkness; the only use of the keys is to penetrate the lock; bread is worthless until it penetrates the body; water penetrates the hard crust of the earth; leaven penetrates the dough, to make it rise . . . . [3]

This kind of investment is necessary if we are to have the kind of teaching ministry Jesus had.

End Notes

[1] Helmut Thielicke, *The Waiting Father* (New York: Harper and Row, Publishers, Inc., 1975), 88-89.

[2] For more information about the FAITH Sunday School Evangelism Strategy®, call toll free 1-877-324-8498. To register for a FAITH Training Clinic, call toll free 1-800-254-2022.

[3] Elton Trueblood, *The Company of the Committed* (San Francisco: Harper and Row, Publishers, 1961), 68.

Jesus Had a Plan. Do We?

Jesus did not approach His life and ministry haphazardly. His mission was far too important. He gave His best; He gave His all. His approach and *method* were appropriate for the time, setting, and people to whom He related.

As a result, people characterized His teaching as new, authoritative, and different from the teaching they heard from others. Those who received Jesus and His message were transformed. The transformation was spiritual but evidence of the change could be seen in the external practices and personal character of those who experienced it.

What were some elements of His plan? Can those elements be part of our plan? Read on.

Jesus Had a Plan

In terms of style, we may tend to think of Jesus as an itinerant teacher. That assessment is true if we mean that He moved from place to place, did not lead or have an association with a teaching-learning institution, or was not a published author. It is not true if we mean Jesus' ministry just happened or that He lacked a plan.

Jesus was part of a plan, a long-range plan that originated in the mind of God the Father (Eph. 1:3-10). The goal of the plan was redemption and the unification of all things in Christ. This plan was to be revealed or implemented according to God's own timing (Gal. 4:4). It will be consummated in God's own time as well (Acts 1:7).

In earlier pages we have seen how Jesus approached His ministry. He moved in response to His call. What He did was intentional and purposeful. His message was clear. His focus on people was obvious. Now review some other aspects of Jesus' ministry that were part of His plan for doing what the Father had sent Him to do—transform lives.

Jesus Cultivated People

Jesus drew people to Himself. His personality, dynamism, and message attracted masses like a magnet pulls steel shavings to itself. He was interested in people, all people, all kinds of people. But Jesus was not just interested in drawing a crowd. He did not gauge His effectiveness by the number of people who came to Him. In fact, He knew crowds could be fickle.

What Jesus wanted was to cultivate followers, for He had plans for them. He called people to Himself in order to send them out. That is seen in the setting aside of the twelve. "The plan was that they would be with him, and he would send them out to proclaim the Word and give them authority to banish demons" (Mark 3:14-15). Similarly, "later the Master selected seventy and sent them ahead of him in pairs to every town and place where he intended to go" (Luke 10:1). He called them, He instructed them (Matt. 10:1—11:1), and He sent them out. Apparently He had confidence in them. He would not always be with them, but in the power of the Holy Spirit those whom He called would be charged to declare the gospel at home and around the world (Matt. 28:19-20; Acts 1:8). Using that methodology, the plan of God for redemption would continue to be declared.

Jesus Presented the Message

We already have seen how critical the message was that Jesus came to declare. And it must be declared with clarity. While the miracles He performed drew much attention, Jesus had settled the issue in the wilderness, when He declared to the tempter, "It takes more than bread to stay alive. It takes a steady stream of words from God's mouth" (Matt. 4:4). Or when He said to the disciples who informed Him everyone was looking for Him, "Let's go to the rest of the villages so I can preach there also. This is why I've come" (Mark 1:38).

Jesus Modeled the Message

One clear example is Jesus' washing the disciples' feet the night of His last Passover supper with them. After completing what was regarded as a task reserved for the lowliest of servants, Jesus said: "Do you understand what I have done to you? You address me as 'Teacher' and 'Master,' and rightly so. That is what I am. So if I, the Master and Teacher, washed your feet, you must now wash each other's feet. I've laid down a pattern for you. What I've done, you do" (John 13:12-15). Jesus not only taught a lesson, He also offered Himself as the lesson.

Jesus Used a Variety of Teaching Approaches

As far as we know Jesus did not study teaching methodology, yet He clearly was a master who skillfully used the method appropriate for the moment. Space will only allow us to survey some of the approaches Jesus took.

Stories.—A skilled storyteller, Jesus is most often identified with this teaching method. Beyond the spiritual value of His stories, some are regarded as literary masterpieces. Some of His stories may have been factual accounts of actual events; others may have been realistic illustrations with which His hearers could identify.

Some of Jesus' most familiar stories are "The Prodigal Son" (Luke 15:11-32); "The Good Samaritan" (Luke 10:29-37); and "The Parable of the Sower" (Matt 13:1-9).

Objects.—To make truth concrete in the minds of His hearers, sometimes Jesus used objects to illustrate the lesson. He pointed to a child to illustrate His teaching about the attitude one should have toward the kingdom of God (Matt. 18:1-4). While teaching outdoors, He may have pointed to the birds flying overhead or picked a flower from the field to support His teaching about the provision of God (Matt. 6:25-30).

Drama.—Jesus didn't produce plays but He did engage in dramatic action to make a point. We already have alluded to His washing of the disciples' feet as an example of humble service (John 13). The Lord's Supper became a dramatic portrayal of the sacrificial intent of His death (Luke 22:14-20). His entry into Jerusalem riding on the foal of a donkey was a dramatic way of identifying Himself with the king of peace spoken of by the prophets (Mark 11:1-10; Zech. 9:9-11).

Discussion.—Most often Jesus employed this method with individuals more than in group settings. In using this teaching approach Jesus was able to present the message concurrently with the individual's processing what he or she was hearing. Jesus' encounter with Nicodemus (John 3), His conversation with the Samaritan woman (John 4), and His public dialogue with the rich, young ruler (Matt. 19:16-22) are examples of discussion.

Questions and Answers.—One of the oldest teaching methods in pedagogy, the question and answer approach is a valuable way to get and hold the attention of the learner, provoke thought, and clarify impressions. We first see Jesus engaged in questions and answers as a 12-year-old boy in Jerusalem (Luke 2:46). He used

this approach with His disciples on the retreat in Caesarea Philippi
(Matt. 16:13-17); with James and John in responding to their
request for a place of honor in the kingdom (Mark 10:35-40); and
as a way to confront the inquiring scribe with the truth taught in
the story of the Good Samaritan.

Lecture.—Yes, Jesus even used lecture. His discourses, which
covered a variety of subjects, were delivered to large crowds (John
6:25-59); large crowds and His disciples (Matt. 5—7); and to the
disciples alone (John 14—17).

Jesus Was Innovative

Jesus' innovativeness is seen in that He broke with the formalities
often associated with teaching or associated with most teachers of
His day. He was not formally trained, He was not part of a
recognized teaching-learning institution, nor did He espouse a
particular pedagogical theory. Yet He taught effectively with
authority. His teaching made a difference as evidenced in the lives
that were transformed.

He taught anytime. Bible teaching for Jesus was not limited to
9:45 Sunday morning. Sharing such an urgent message could not
be limited to a particular time. For Jesus, teaching time was
whenever a person or a crowd was present. So, He taught
Nicodemus at night (John 3:2); the Samaritan woman at noon (John
4:6); a crowd in the temple at dawn (John 8:2). Some of His
teaching would appear to take place in brief encounters (Mark
2:18-20). However, two disciples of John the Baptizer apparently
spent the day learning from Jesus (John 1:35-40).

He taught anyplace. He did teach in the synagogue (Luke 4:14-
22), but again He was not limited to formal settings. His classroom
was the world. Hence, His teaching lectern may have been a rock
or grassy place on the mountainside (Matt. 5:1), a boat on the
seashore (Luke 5:3), or a dusty road (Luke 24:13-32).

He used the resources He had at hand. With no particular time
or place for teaching, Jesus did not have the resources for teaching
immediately at hand. Yet with the world as His classroom, He was

not at a loss for teaching aids and resources.

He used what was around Him—the birds, flowers, little children, a mustard seed—to illustrate the eternal truths that could transform lives. Even if an object was not in hand, Jesus alluded to situations with which people were familiar—a farmer planting seed, cultivating the ground, and harvesting the crop. He spoke of common elements like bread, yeast, light, fish, nets, and water.

In part, Jesus' innovativeness was spurred by His spontaneity. Jesus was always the Teacher. He did more than present a lesson; He modeled the lesson. He didn't wait for a class to gather, but he seized the moment that came with an encounter with someone crying out in need (Luke 7:9-15), an inquiry by a confused follower (Luke 7:18-23), or even a personal criticism (Luke 7:36-50).

Once again, we affirm that He was successful. His success is seen in the testimony of those who first heard Him. On one occasion in Capernaum where Jesus spent the day teaching, "They were surprised at his teaching—so forthright, so confident—not quibbling and quoting like the religion scholars. . . . Everyone there was incredulous, buzzing with curiosity. 'What's going on here? A new teaching that does what it says?' " (Mark 1:22,27).

His success is seen in the affirmation of the Father. Jesus said His words and deeds were one with the Father (John 14:10-11). The Father, in turn, gave approval to His Son through His words (Matt. 17:5) and through the power of the resurrection (Acts 2:32-36).

Jesus' success is seen in the myriad of lives that have been transformed by a faith response to Him and His redemptive message. The past and present is replete with stories of those who have become new in Christ and have devoted themselves to being teachers of His truth.

Jesus had a plan. His plan was the Father's plan. It worked—and is working!

Do You Have a Plan?

Many leaders just do not like to plan. They are good at dreaming and envisioning. They make great resolutions and have the best of intentions. Nevertheless, they can't or won't make the kind of preparation essential for bringing dreams to fruition. If we want different results, then we must do the kinds of things that lead to those results.

The work we are about is God's work, not our work. Therefore, we can't make it happen. It is not under our control—if it is, then it may just be our work. We must rely on the dynamic movement of His Holy Spirit to inspire our dreaming, influence the actions we take, and empower our doing. Yet none of this is an excuse for idleness. He has commissioned us to action—make disciples—not to sky-gazing (Matt. 28:19; Acts 1:8-11). Our faith in Jesus' return is to move us into action, so that all will be ready to receive Him.

A church that takes seriously and personally the commission of Christ, has determined that Sunday School is its foundational strategy, and has adopted transformational teaching as a best practice needs to approach its work with intentionality. It is too urgent for a haphazard, traditional repetitive, or even the easiest approach. A plan must be set in place that accomplishes the purpose. A plan requires planning.

More extensive help for developing an annual plan for your Sunday School ministry can be found in the resources in the *Sunday School for a New Century* series. These leadership development resources provide information concerning leader enlistment, organizing the ministry, developing an annual plan, and implementing the strategy. A monthly magazine, *The Sunday School Leader,* addresses issues of interest to the general Sunday School leader and provides practical help and ideas for all areas of Sunday School ministry.

Let's look back at the elements of Jesus' ministry we just considered. This time, however, look at them from the perspective of your Sunday School ministry.

Is Your Sunday School Ministry Cultivating People?

Without minimizing the importance of gathering as many people as possible as participants in Bible study, remember, assembling a crowd is not the ultimate goal. The goal is that each person will be transformed by the power of the Holy Spirit and become engaged in kingdom ministry through the church. A transformational teaching ministry seeks to reach, equip, and mobilize its members for service. The success of a teacher, especially an Adult Sunday School class teacher, is best measured by the number of persons in the class who either leave the class for a leadership role, become part of a core group to begin a new unit, or are leaders in other ministries of the church.

Ask these questions:

• How many new leaders were enlisted this past year?

• How many new Bible study groups did we begin this year using a core group from an existing Bible study group?

• How many new members have been enrolled in each class and department?

• How many members in each class or department are also participants in ongoing discipleship training?

• How many members in each class or department are serving as leaders in other church ministries?

Based on your responses to these questions, on a scale of 1 to 5 (with 5 being high), how would you rate your Sunday School ministry in terms of its cultivating people? _____

Determine goals for next year and some actions you can lead your Sunday School ministry to take to achieve them.

Is Your Sunday School Ministry Presenting the Message?

Many good things can take place in and through a Sunday School class or department. Even so, Bible study should be prominent. The message must be taught. Prayer, as important as it is to our spiritual development, should not take away from the Bible study time. Fellowship, as valuable as it is in enhancing our relationships, should not take away from an encounter with God's Word. The time set aside for Bible study should not be encroached upon by program promotions or project planning. The Bible study group is not the place for presenting personal opinions about current events or discussing other topics, no matter how good or important they they are. If we invite people to Bible study, advertise Sunday School ministry as Bible study, and declare that we strongly believe in Bible study, then we are compelled to provide Bible study.

A critical part of presenting the message is having a Bible study curriculum that is trustworthy and true to Holy Scripture and meets the needs of the users. There are two aspects of curriculum: the curriculum plan and the curriculum resources. The curriculum plan sets the course for what is studied. The curriculum resources contain the curriculum plan and set forth how to study it.

What guidelines should you use to select or develop an ongoing curriculum plan for your church, and why will such a plan keep you on an exciting and fruitful track?

1. *When choosing a curriculum plan, choose one that covers all of the Bible's content, not just selected or "favorite" parts.*

2. *Choose a plan that has a balance of biblical content, Bible study approaches, and life issues.* For example, the plan should contain a balance of Old Testament studies, the life of Christ, and New Testament epistles. The plan could contain a balance of approaches to studying the Bible, such as studying through a book of the Bible, a character in the Bible, or a topic or life issue in the Bible.

Why not just choose whatever people want to study, or whatever the "hot topic" or "felt need" is? By following a systematic, comprehensive plan, ongoing Bible study points repeatedly to the fact that the Bible, not developmental life needs and human issues, must guide and shape believers' lives.

If a Sunday School leader selects studies that only address age-group needs and issues, then the leader risks supplanting the Bible's goal for believers with contemporary perceptions of age-group needs and issues. Occasional topical, issue-oriented studies are necessary and included in ongoing curriculum plans, but the ultimate goal of the Bible and Sunday School curriculum is to lead people toward faith in Christ and transformation toward Christlikeness.

While He was responsive to immediate physical, emotional, and spiritual needs, Jesus did not always teach on subjects the people wanted—their "felt needs." Jesus was aware there were deeper issues of the human heart that went beyond the current issues of the day—ceremonial washing of hands, Sabbath laws, and getting caught in adultery. Jesus' curriculum plan focused on redemption, the cross, and transformation of human lives beginning with the human heart.

Make sure the plan has a balanced diet of biblical truth and life issues; a curriculum plan needs to address head-on where people are. However, a balanced curriculum plan will not only address the "hot topics" and "felt needs" but also studies that place people on the race toward mature biblical faith, such as being in Christ, being empowered by the Holy Spirit, being a faithful witness, caring for a lost world, and developing a biblical worldview.

3. Confirm that the curriculum plan is properly sequenced so that learners can build on what they already know. A systematic approach to Bible study facilitates the integration of biblical truth into the learner's life as a lifelong ongoing process. Jesus built on what His hearers already knew and took them to a new level when He said, "You have heard that it was said . . . But I tell you . . . ." (Matt. 5:43-44, NIV).

At the same time, open Bible study groups will always have new people joining the curriculum race—new learners who need the basics the veteran learners could help teach. Do a quick survey of Jesus' teaching in the Gospels, and you will discover how frequently He repeated themes—and how slowly His disciples caught on.

A properly sequenced Bible study plan is one expression of the principle of renewing the mind found in Romans 12:2. The ministry of the Holy Spirit is one of helping believers recall what Jesus taught, of helping believers become "experts" in living and in bearing witness for Christ. Curriculum can support your goals for transformational Bible study.

4. *A planned, ongoing Bible study strategy is most conducive to creating a ministry environment that fosters strong relationships and regularly invites the lost to believe in Christ.* One important aspect of creating a ministry environment is helping prepare the participants to hear God's message for a particular time. A planned, ongoing Bible study strategy is a wise discipline for the person who wants to hear God speak and is seeking to obey God's direction. By submitting to a disciplined, lifelong approach to listening to God through His written Word, we do not presume to know exactly what God would speak to us. Instead we demonstrate a commitment to love God and His Word—all of it; to trust God and His Word—-all of it; and to obey God and His Word—all of it. Teaching and studying an ongoing, well-designed curriculum plan demonstrates a heart that is ready to be transformed.

With regard to the curriculum resources, make sure the resources you choose express the curriculum plan that meets these four principles and accomplishes the ministry goals you and your church believe God wants you to fulfill. Materials produced by LifeWay Christian Resources contain Bible study curriculum plans that are comprehensive, balanced, properly sequenced, and conducive to ongoing ministry and address the 1•5•4 Principle of Kingdom Growth. In addition, LifeWay curriculum resources, whether print, video, audio, electronic, or multimedia—

- guide churches to fulfill the Great Commission through the five essential functions for church growth—evangelism, discipleship, fellowship, ministry, and worship;

• provide sound, reliable interpretation of the Bible from a conservative point of view;

• offer clear support for evangelism, including the FAITH Sunday School Evangelism Strategy®;

• provide a variety of age-appropriate, timely, and relevant teaching-learning approaches, all of which lead learners toward faith in Christ and spiritual transformation into Christlikeness;

• supplement teaching-learning plans with resource kits and leader packs containing creative posters and teaching aids and free online *EXTRA!* teaching supplements containing the latest in news, research, and ideas on this Web site, www.lifeway.com;

• provide choices of Bible study options that feature comprehensive, balanced, sequenced, and ministry-conducive curriculum;

• offer a variety of reasonably priced, easy-to-use, and attractive learner and leader resources in print, audio, electronic, and/or multimedia formats;

• feature biblical insights and teaching approaches written by Southern Baptists who are experienced in Sunday School ministry in churches;

• provide financial assistance for various Southern Baptist ministries;

• offer an optional devotional and reading guide to deepen participants' daily commitment to love, trust, and obey God based on the Bible study participants study on Sunday; and

• contain leader, teacher, and learner development features to engage and equip persons in the full ministry of evangelism, discipleship, fellowship, ministry, and worship through Sunday School ministry.

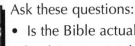

Ask these questions:

• Is the Bible actually a prominent part of our Sunday School ministry? Why or why not?

• Do we provide training so our leaders are well equipped for Bible teaching?

• Do we provide strong, Bible-based curriculum materials and teaching resources to members and leaders?
• Do we talk about the discipline of Bible study and aggressively work to lead church members and guests into a Bible study group?
• Do we encourage learners to use their Bibles?

 Based on your responses to these questions, on a scale of 1 to 5 (with 5 being high), how would you rate your Sunday School ministry in terms of its faithfulness in presenting the message? _____

Determine goals for next year and some actions you can lead your Sunday School ministry to take to achieve them.

Are Your Sunday School Leaders Modeling the Message?

Some teachers may be eloquent presenters, experts in Bible knowledge, and experienced in teaching methodology and technique, but not the kind of teachers who are effective in teaching for spiritual transformation. Why?

Because they teach the lesson but do not model it. Therefore, they have no credibility with those whom they are trying to teach. The lesson becomes material but not life.

Take a lesson on worship, for example. The teacher may present the material to class members well. However, the class members seldom see the teacher in worship. How effective can that teacher be? Not very. On the other hand, a teacher who is known to be regular in private and public worship will be able to teach about worship from a true-to-life perspective.

Ask these questions:
- Are the leaders in your Sunday School ministry perceived as practitioners of disciplines of the faith: public worship, Bible reading, prayer, stewardship, evangelism, personal spiritual growth, ministry, and so forth?
- Are intentional actions taken to communicate this expectation to potential leaders? Are current leaders held accountable for being models of faithful living?

Based on your responses to these questions, on a scale of 1 to 5 (with 5 being high), how would you rate your Sunday School ministry in terms of its leaders being models of the message? _____

Determine goals for next year and some actions you can lead your Sunday School ministry to take to achieve them.

Do Your Sunday School Leaders Use a Variety of Teaching Approaches?

Why did Jesus use a variety of teaching approaches in His ministry? Because God created people with different ways of learning and dealing with life situations.

With Jesus as model, the Sunday School teacher has the strategic role of selecting ways to communicate the message that reflects knowledge of learners and their varied approaches to learning. The role of the teacher is to create an environment and guide learning in ways that will facilitate the work of the Holy Spirit and will encourage learners to experience spiritual transformation.

This role includes recognizing the varied ways learners approach learning and their individual level of learning. To ensure that all learners encounter the message, teachers of all age groups must use methods that incorporate several approaches. A teacher should evaluate how well he or she achieves the teaching objectives of specific lessons, especially the spiritual transformation goals of laying foundations, leading people to faith, and guiding them to grow in Christlikeness.

While God created every person to be unique, there are some common ways people of all ages approach learning. These approaches include *relational, musical, logical, natural, physical, reflective, visual,* and *verbal.* While every person has a dominant approach to learning, he or she can learn through multiple approaches, often simultaneously.

In the following paragraphs, each approach is described in brief detail and an example of a Bible person who represents this approach to learning and teaching is given.

Relational

These learners are highly social people, make friends easily, and may be very good talkers. They are keen observers of others, noticing their moods and motivations. Recognizing how people feel enables relational individuals to respond accordingly. They are drawn to activities that allow them to cooperate and interact with others. They may be known as "people persons."

In Acts, Joseph of Cyprus was soon renamed Barnabas "the encourager" because of the way he related to the church, its ministry, and to other Christians like John Mark.

Musical

Many people enjoy music. Some people seem more sensitive to rhythm and pitch than others. They tend to be good listeners. Because they are comfortable with music, singing and movement are their natural responses to music. These learners may learn new songs quickly and remember them easily. They find it easy to express themselves through composing, playing, and performing.

As David penned his psalms, he expressed his faith in a musical form. His words form the basis for many contemporary choruses and hymns of praise.

Logical

Problem-solving is an enjoyable experience for some learners. They see patterns in the world and can reason through difficult situations. These learners rely heavily on analogies. They like working with abstractions and may be gifted in the field of mathematics. They enjoy games and puzzles.

When making a point to his readers, Paul often used a very logical argument or formal debate style. He stated evidence from the Old Testament. He appealed to logic and reason in matters of grace and faith. The Book of Romans is an excellent example of approaching learning and teaching through logic.

Natural

These learners enjoy the beauty of God's creation. They are skilled at identifying elements of the natural world. They may relate well to stories in the Bible that allude to elements in nature. Investigation and exploration of God's world are appealing to these learners. They have a fascination for plants and animals and a high sensitivity for the stewardship of God's world.

Many of the psalms approach teaching and learning from a sensitivity to the natural world. Psalm 8, 23, and 139 all are examples of David's experience with God and His mighty works. David saw God active in nature all around him.

Physical

Persons who approach learning from a physical standpoint are very active and may have good coordination. When they tell a story, they not only tell it, they also play it out. Physical learners may be inclined to learn through mission projects or other helping activities. They like to use their physical abilities and skills in sports and drama.

Ezekiel has been described as an ecstatic kind of prophet. His unique approach to "forth telling" and "foretelling" drew great attention during his ministry. He acted out many of his prophesies to make points that were memorable for his contemporaries.

Reflective

Reflective learners tend to understand who they are and how they feel. Working alone may be their desire. People who have this approach to learning do not shun the company of others but often choose activities that allow self-expression. These people also are comfortable with extended periods of solitude. They may internalize concepts by personalizing them.

During the significant times in the life of Mary, the Gospels portray her as a woman who pondered God's will and her role in His plan. She found times of reflection to be her own personal teachable moments.

Visual

Visual learners can "see" in their imaginations as well as in the concrete world. Their visual understanding includes space and distance concepts. They also enjoy creating their own pictures and visual representations of what they are learning. Visual arts, videos, television, and film foster productive means of learning for these individuals.

John, as he wrote both the Gospel, epistles, and Revelation, used vivid images to paint pictures for his readers. Light and darkness were just two elements John used to teach his followers about God and godliness.

Verbal

Some people learn best through words—reading, writing, speaking, and listening. Verbal learners like the sounds of words and may have large vocabularies. People with this approach to learning like to talk and play word games. They enjoy stories, poems, debates, speeches, and essays.

Solomon represents an individual who approached learning from a verbal perspective. His speech at the dedication of the temple (1 Kings 8) demonstrates a verbal approach to learning.

Knowing the learning approaches preferred by one's learners will influence selection of the method(s) used in the learning situation.

Methods are the tools a teacher uses to engage the learner. Use of different methods in the same teaching session opens the possibilities of engaging people who take different approaches to learning. The chart in Appendix C overviews the approaches to learning and gives examples of some methods that could be employed. Notice that some methods may be more appropriate for some age groups than others.

Ask these questions:
• Do the leaders understand the age group they teach and use methods appropriate to them?
• Do leaders vary their approaches to teaching or generally rely upon one?
• Is regular training provided to help leaders develop teaching skills?
• Generally, what percentage of leaders are willing to attend regularly leadership team meetings? Leadership training sessions?

Based on your responses to these questions, on a scale of 1 to 5 (with 5 being high), how would you rate your Sunday School ministry in terms of its use of a variety of teaching approaches and methods? _____

Determine goals for next year and some actions you can lead your Sunday School ministry to take to achieve them.

Is Your Sunday School Ministry Innovative?

This question is subject to misunderstanding. To introduce something new, as *innovation* suggests, does not mean discarding the old. Something new may be added without deleting that which has been the tradition. On the other hand, we are not to be so bound to the tradition that we cannot discard it when it is no longer useful. The struggle of people to cling to the traditions was an issue Jesus faced often in His confrontations with the religious leaders of His day. They came to think the traditions were equal to divine truth and revelation— thinking which Jesus challenged (Mark 7:1-13).

Innovative thinking about Sunday School expands the ministry beyond what it may currently be on Sunday morning. Sunday School ministry can include Bible study groups that meet anytime, anyplace, if those groups are aimed at fulfilling the purpose of Sunday School ministry. You may need to develop multiple meeting times on Sunday or meet on Saturday evening. The possibilities are as big as your dreams and commitment to reach people for Christ. Look again at the definition for Sunday School given on page 12 of this book.

 Ask these questions:
• If we are to continue to reach people, engage in a vital ministry of transformational teaching, and expand our kingdom work, do we need to look for other ways and seize the new opportunities that are around us?
• Is our Sunday School leadership team willing to break the bonds of tradition to develop Bible study groups anytime, anyplace that reach people groups heretofore unreached?

Based on your responses to these questions, on a scale of 1 to 5 (with 5 being high), how would you rate your Sunday School ministry in terms of its willingness to be innovative—at least in the sense Jesus was innovative? _____

Determine goals for next year and some actions you can lead your Sunday School ministry to take to achieve them.

Conclusion

Teaching the Jesus way—what a challenge! It means teaching with a sense of call as a child of God. It means teaching for spiritual transformation. It means teaching a message clearly from God's Holy Word. It means teaching with a willingness to invest oneself in others. It means teaching with a plan

Are you feeling overwhelmed? Do you wonder whether this type of teaching can be done in your setting? Those feelings are not uncommon. However, the assurance we have is that teaching the Jesus way is not something we do on our own, under our own power. He who has all authority has commissioned us to the task. He has promised us His presence. That changes things. That changes us, too. We are able to teach the Jesus way when we are under His authority and filled with power of His presence.

Think once again about these words from Romans: "Fix your attention on God. You'll be changed from the inside out. Readily recognize what he wants from you, and quickly respond to it. Unlike the culture around you, always dragging you down to its level of immaturity, God brings the best out of you, develops well-formed maturity in you" (Rom. 12:2). Only then can you build a ministry that teaches for spiritual transformation. Only then can you and those you lead teach the Jesus way.

Prepared by God to S.E.R.V.E.

Leaders know who they are in Christ Jesus. They know how God has molded and gifted them for His use. They trust that God can use every experience to prepare them for ministry. They trust that God has prepared them to serve for His glory, not their gain.

God has prepared you for His purposes to bring honor to Him. The Bible says to use the spiritual gifts God gave you to serve others (1 Pet. 4:10). Servant leaders are leaders who serve. The acrostic *S.E.R.V.E.* is an outline for how God has prepared you for His purposes.

S piritual gifts— Those gifts God gives through His Holy Spirit to empower you for service

E xperiences— Those events God allows which mold you into a servant leader

R elational style— Behavioral traits God uses to give you a leadership style

V ocational skills— Those abilities you have gained through training and experience which you can use in service to God

E nthusiasm— That passion God has put in your heart for a certain ministry to others

Your relationship with Christ as well as these five areas—spiritual gifts, experiences, relational style, vocational skills, and enthusiasm—become the raw materials God uses to mold you into a servant leader.

Spiritual Gifts

A spiritual gift is a "manifestation of the Spirit" (1 Cor. 12:7, NIV). It is not a special ability you develop on your own; that is a skill or talent. You do not seek a spiritual gift. But you should prayerfully seek to understand how God already has gifted you for His purposes.

The church works best when its members know how God has gifted them spiritually and when all members, empowered by their spiritual gifts, are in places of service. Spiritual gifts are the key to understanding how God intends the church to function. Understanding spiritual gifts begins with knowing the biblical nature of the church.

Both 1 Corinthians 12:7 and Ephesians 4:12 help us understand why God gives gifts to the church. "Now to each one the manifestation of the Spirit is given for the common good" (1 Cor. 12:7, NIV). Ephesians 4:12 (NIV) further describes this purpose: "To prepare God's people for works of service, so that the body of Christ may be built up." Spiritual gifts are for the common good of the church. God gifts members of the church to equip and build up the body of Christ.

Important to any study of spiritual gifts is God's work in the life of the believer and the church. You do not decide you want a certain gift and then go get it. God gives the gifts "just as he determines" (1 Cor. 12:11, NIV). Spiritual gifts are part of God's design for a person's life and for the life of the church. The Bible says that "God has arranged the parts in the body, every one of them, just as he wanted them to be" (1 Cor. 12:18, NIV). Your goal as a servant leader is to discover how God in His grace has gifted you for service, and to lead others in the same joy of discovery.

Ken Hemphill defines a spiritual gift as "an individual manifestation of grace from the Father that enables you to serve Him and thus play a vital role in His plan for the redemption of the world."[1] For S.E.R.V.E, we will use this definition: *A spiritual gift is an expression of the Holy Spirit in the life of believers which empowers them to serve the body of Christ, the church.* Romans 12:6-8; 1 Corinthians 12:8-10,28-30; Ephesians 4:11; and 1 Peter 4:9-11 contain representative lists of gifts/roles God has given to the church, and brief definitions follow. Check the gifts that seem to fit how God has made you.

- *Leadership*—Leadership aids the body by leading and directing members to accomplish the goals and purposes of the church. Leadership motivates people to work together in unity toward common goals (Rom. 12:8).
- *Administration*—Persons with the gift of administration lead the body by steering others to remain on task. Administration enables the body to organize according to God-given purposes and long-term goals (1 Cor. 12:28).
- *Teaching*—Teaching is instructing members in the truths and doctrines of God's Word for the purposes of building up, unifying, and maturing the body (1 Cor. 12:28; Rom. 12:7; Eph. 4:11).
- *Knowledge*—The gift of knowledge manifests itself in teaching and training in discipleship. It is the God-given ability to learn, know, and explain the truths of God's Word. A word of knowledge is a Spirit-revealed truth (1 Cor. 12:28).
- *Wisdom*—Wisdom is the gift that discerns the work of the Holy Spirit in the body and applies His teachings/actions to the needs of the body (1 Cor. 12:28).
- *Prophecy*—The gift of prophecy is proclaiming the Word of God boldly. This builds up the body and leads to conviction of sin. Prophecy manifests itself in preaching and teaching (1 Cor. 12:10; Rom. 12:6).
- *Discernment*—Discernment aids the body by recognizing the true intentions of those within or related to the body. Discernment tests the message and actions of others for the protection and well-being of the body (1 Cor. 12:10).
- *Exhortation*—Possessors of this gift encourage members to be involved in and enthusiastic about the work of the Lord. Members with this gift are good counselors and motivate others to service. Exhortation exhibits itself in preaching, teaching, and ministry (Rom. 12:8).
- *Shepherding*—The gift of shepherding is manifested in persons who look out for the spiritual welfare of others. Although pastors, like shepherds, care for members of the church, this gift is not limited to a pastor or staff member (Eph. 4:11).
- *Faith*—Faith trusts God to work beyond the human capabilities of the people. Believers with this gift encourage others to trust in God in the face of apparently insurmountable odds (1 Cor. 12:9).
- *Evangelism*—God gifts his church with evangelists to lead others to Christ effectively and enthusiastically. This gift builds up the body by adding new members to its fellowship (Eph. 4:11).
- *Apostleship*—The church sends apostles from the body to plant churches or be

missionaries. Apostles motivate the body to look beyond its walls in order to carry out the Great Commission (1 Cor. 12:28; Eph. 4:11).

• *Service/Helps*—Those with the gift of service/helps recognize practical needs in the body and joyfully give assistance to meeting those needs. Christians with this gift do not mind working behind the scenes (1 Cor. 12:28; Rom. 12:7).

• *Mercy*—Cheerful acts of compassion characterize those with the gift of mercy. Persons with this gift aid the body by empathizing with hurting members. They keep the body healthy and unified by keeping others aware of the needs within the church (Rom. 12:8).

• *Giving*—Members with the gift of giving give freely and joyfully to the work and mission of the body. Cheerfulness and liberality are characteristics of individuals with this gift (Rom. 12:8).

• *Hospitality*—Those with this gift have the ability to make visitors, guests, and strangers feel at ease. They often use their home to entertain guests. Persons with this gift integrate new members into the body (1 Pet. 4:9).

List here the gifts you have begun to discover in your life:

1._____

2._____

3._____

God has gifted you with an expression of His Holy Spirit to support His vision and mission of the church—a worldwide vision to reach all people with the gospel of Christ. God has gifted you for service in Christ's body, the church (1 Cor. 12:7). His goal is for you to prepare others for service in the church (Eph. 4:12). As a servant leader, you are to use your spiritual gifts for the common good of the body. God gifted you for His glory, not your gain. God gifted you to build up His church, not your ego.

After prayer and worship, I am beginning to sense that God wants me to use my spiritual gifts to serve Christ's body by . . .

I am not sure yet how God wants me to use my gifts to serve others. But I am committed to prayer and worship, seeking wisdom and opportunities to use the gifts I have received from God.

Experiences

Leaders trust that God works in their lives to bring about His plan for their lives. Experiences become God's crucible to mold you into His image. Servant leaders are confident that events which happen to them and around them are part of God's sovereign work in creation.

God can take what already has happened in your life to help accomplish His will. God can mold and make you into a tool of His grace. God can break into your life to make you a new creation for His purposes.

Henry Blackaby calls events like Paul's conversion "spiritual markers." He says a spiritual marker "identifies a time of transition, decision, or direction when I clearly know that God has guided me."[2] Spiritual markers remind you that God is at work in your history. Remembering them helps you see God's work in your life and how He is unfolding His plan for your life.

You have events in your life when God has made His will clear to you. God broke into history, and you know God spoke to you. He may have confirmed a decision you had made. He may have revealed something new about who He is.

Take a moment to describe in the space below some of your most important encounters with God. Write as if you are telling a friend about these life-changing moments. Start with your salvation experience. Don't worry if you do not have a dramatic desert story. God works in everyday events to shape you into His likeness. Spiritual markers can be any life experience, from a burning bush to a child's gentle touch.

Let me tell you about my most important encounters with God . . .

Relational Style

Every person has a natural style of how he or she relates to others. Every style has its strengths and weaknesses. God can use any relational style that is submitted to His will to serve His purposes.

How you relate is basic to how you serve as a leader. To know your relational style is to know how God has molded you to serve people through your relationships with them. Servant leaders know how they naturally relate to others and how others relate to them.

Since leadership involves influencing others for the common good, knowing how God has molded your temperament is key to knowing your leadership style. Knowing the style of others' also allows you to meet their relational needs. Moreover, understanding the relational needs of others helps you communicate with and lead them more effectively.

God will help you understand your role as a servant leader as you assess the strengths and weaknesses of your relational style. A four-category model has been proven over time and has strong scientific support. The primary source for understanding this model is Ken Voges, an author of *Understanding How Others Misunderstand You.* Voges uses the letters DISC to represent the four primary relational styles.[3]

• **D** stands for the "dominance" style—Works toward achieving goals and results; functions best in active, challenging environments.

• **I** stands for the "influencing" style—Works toward relating to people through verbal persuasion; functions best in friendly, favorable environments.

• **S** is the "steadiness" style—Works toward supporting and cooperating with others; functions best in supportive, harmonious environments.

• **C** represents the "conscientious" style—Works toward doing things right and focuses on details; functions best in structured, orderly environments.

Using the descriptions that best describe you, personalize your DISC style by completing the following statements:

Because of my special, God-given style of relating to others, I tend to work toward . . .

and I function best in . . .

But I also see these additional qualities of my God-given personality:

The most important part of the above activity is to reflect on these questions: *How does my relational style relate to servant leadership? How can my own God-given temperament be used by God to make a difference in my church and community?* Note the following chart that summarizes possible strengths and weaknesses of each leadership style.

Dominant		Influencing	
Strengths	*Weaknesses*	*Strengths*	*Weaknesses*
Direct	Too controlling	Gregarious	Forgets the goal
Active	Hates routine	Enthusiastic	Poor follow-through
Decisive	Hates details	Extremely flexible	Overlooks details
Steadiness		**Conscientious**	
Strengths	*Weaknesses*	*Strengths*	*Weaknesses*
Cooperative	Fails to confront	Detailed	Inflexible
Deliberate	Dislikes change	Conscientious	Rigid
Supportive	Too compromising	Cautious	Indecisive

Note that each style has strengths and weaknesses. No single style can meet every need. God intentionally created a variety of styles, none being more important or more needed than another. All gifts and strengths are important to the overall servant ministry of your church. At the same time, each strength, when out of control, can become a weakness. And weaknesses should not become excuses for failure. A person and a church must strive to accomplish without excuse the ministries received from God.

This diversity of styles within the church may at times produce conflict, but it provides the important balance needed to accomplish what God gives the church to do. It reminds us of the important lesson that God needs each one of us, and that we need each other.

Churches function best when members accept the relational styles of others and seek to meet the needs of those persons, never compromising the message of Christ. Relationships remain strong when members follow God's pattern for living together as His body with all its diversity (1 Cor. 12:14-26).

God's Word offers clear teaching on how we are to serve one another in love. Colossians 3:12-14 (NIV) says, "Therefore, as God's chosen people, holy and dearly loved, clothe yourselves with compassion, kindness, humility, gentleness and patience. Bear with each other and forgive whatever grievances you may have against one another. Forgive as the Lord forgave you. And over all these virtues put on love, which binds them all together in perfect unity."

Remember that your natural relational style is not an excuse to sin. God's indwelling Spirit balances your natural tendencies with God's temperament. Regardless of your style, the fruit of the Spirit (Gal. 5:22-23) is always a vital part of a servant leader's relationships. God's Spirit molds your temperament for His glory.

Vocational Skills

Our English word *vocation* comes from the Latin word *vocare*, which means "to call." A vocation, then, is what one feels called to do with his or her life. In previous generations, a sense of divine calling was part of a person's place in the world. A vocation was part of God's plan for a person's life. God called, and you responded by gaining the skills necessary to live out that calling.

Vocation has come to mean any profession or occupation. A vocational skill is any ability you have learned that enhances your calling in life.

In today's secular world, people often prefer to use the word *career*. A career is your choice. Instead of looking for God's plan, the world teaches you to choose what you want to do and, then, to plot a course of training to accomplish your career choice. A career, then, is what you choose for yourself.

In the New Testament, Paul encouraged the Christians in Ephesus to "live a life worthy of the calling you have received" (Eph. 4:1, NIV). He was not talking about their jobs. He encouraged them to adopt a lifestyle consistent with who they were in Christ. Calling in the Bible is one's position in Christ, not one's position in the world.

Whatever your vocation, your calling is to live worthy of the salvation God gives you in Christ Jesus. In Colossians, Paul wrote, "Whatever you do, work at it with all your heart, as working for the Lord, not for men. . . . It is the Lord Christ you are serving" (Col. 3:23a-24b, NIV). Whatever you do, God calls you to live like a child of God and to bring honor to God through your actions. It matters less what you do in life than it does what you do with your life.

For the sake of our study, let's define *vocation* as what you do to provide for your needs in society, recognizing God's work in your life to lead you to that choice. Calling is God's call to salvation in Christ Jesus and to a special mission in your life for His purposes.

Vocational skills are those skills you have acquired to do your career and/or hobbies. Let's make an inventory of your skills. Use the following table to do so.

Name of Skill   *How I Use This Skill in My Vocation*

1._____   _____

2._____   _____

3._____   _____

God used Paul's vocational skills for his life's calling. God can do the same for you. Take time to imagine how God can use the skills you listed above for His work of spreading the gospel. For example, if one of your skills is carpentry, you can use that skill to build shelves in your church's preschool rooms or for a local mission or ministry. Be creative as you consider how you can use your skills for the glory of God.

Name of Skill   *How God Can Use This Skill in His Mission*

1._____   _____

2._____   _____

3._____   _____

Enthusiasm

The word *enthusiasm* comes from a Greek word that literally means, "in god." The Greeks believed that a god could enter a person and inspire or enthuse him. Our word enthusiasm takes on the meaning, "God in you." While the Greek word for enthuse is not found in the New Testament, the emphasis on God's presence which energizes the believer is a recurring theme (John 14:20; 20:21-22; Matt. 28:18-20; Acts 1:8).

The Bible is clear that God's Holy Spirit is the source of passion for God's mission within the believer. Paul declared it is "Christ in you" which is "the hope of glory" (Col. 1:27, NIV). We do not generate hope on our own. God energizes us with His living Holy Spirit. Jesus promised that the Holy Spirit will be our Counselor and "guide you into all truth" (John 16:7,13, NIV). He is our counselor and guide as we follow the Lord. Passion and enthusiasm for ministry come from God.

Scripture tells about people who were enthusiastic about what they did. This is not a self-generated thrill. Enthusiasm is a God-given desire to serve Him by meeting the needs of others. Servant leaders have a God-given passion to serve.

A servant leader's joy comes when he sees God at work and he is a part of it. Servant leadership is a God-given passion for the success of God's plan. Servant leaders find joy when God's will is done.

Your God-given enthusiasm is sometimes your only source of joy in ministry. As you lead, you will face obstacles and disappointments. People will criticize you. Sometimes they will question your motives. But the sincere desire to know God's will and the passion God puts in your heart for His work absorb these negative reactions and allow you to move forward with your ministry. Your enthusiasm is the beginning of a fruitful life in Christ.

What has God burned in your heart to do for His mission on earth? Take a moment to consider what that may be. Prayerfully write your responses to the following statements. Complete them with honest, heartfelt statements.

The one thing I do for God that makes my heart beat fast is . . .

If I could do one thing for God, it would be to . . .

My S.E.R.V.E. Profile

Believing God has prepared me for servant leadership. I am discovering that He has molded me in the following areas (Pull together what you have written on previous pages to complete the following statements):

- *God has gifted me with the spiritual gifts of:*

- *God has allowed these experiences to guide me for His purposes:*

- *God has created me to relate most often to others naturally in this way:*

- *God has given me the opportunities to develop these vocational skills that can be used in His service:*

- *God has burned in my heart the enthusiasm to serve in this area of ministry:*

End Notes

"Prepared by God to S.E.R.V.E." has been adapted from C. Gene Wilkes, *Jesus on Leadership: Becoming a Servant Leader* (Nashville: LifeWay Press, 1996), 31-84. This resource can lead you to apply biblical principles of servant leadership to all areas of ministry and includes more detailed spiritual gifts and relational style surveys.

[1] Ken Hemphill, *Serving God: Discovering and Using Your Spiritual Gifts Workbook* (Dallas: The Sampson Company, 1995), 22.

[2] Henry Blackaby and Claude V. King, *Experiencing God: Knowing and Doing the Will of God* (Nashville: Convention Press, 1990), 104.

[3] Ken Voges and Ron Braud, *Understanding How Others Misunderstand You* (Chicago: Moody, 1980).

Common Characteristics of LifeWay Bible Study Resources

A best practice for Sunday School is to choose sound curriculum. Sunday School emphasizes ongoing, open Bible study groups that reproduce new groups as the best long-term approach for building a ministry environment that (1) guides preschoolers/children toward conversion through foundational teaching; (2) encourages unsaved people to come to faith in Christ; (3) assimilates new believers into the church; and (4) encourages believers to lead others to Christ.

Sunday School leaders need to map out Bible study curriculum that causes learners to explore the whole counsel of God during the life stages of the learners. Curriculum is "the continuous course, process, system for Bible study groups to lay foundations for children, to guide unbelievers toward faith in Christ, and to guide believers toward Christlikeness integrating biblical truth into the learner's life." All LifeWay Bible study resources emphasize the following 10 characteristics.

Biblical Authority. — All LifeWay Bible studies champion the Bible as the inerrant and infallible Word of God. All Bible study content affirms the basic Christian beliefs as set forth in *The Baptist Faith and Message.* Bible study materials affirm biblical authority for all of life and for all fields of knowledge; God's direct creation of mankind and the belief that Adam and Eve were real persons; that the named authors wrote the biblical books attributed to them; that the miracles described in Scripture occurred as supernatural events in history; and that the historical narratives by biblical authors are accurate and reliable.

The kingdom of God is present wherever the will and reign of God is established in people's lives through Jesus Christ. The 1-5-4 Principle of church growth states that there is 1 Great Commission, 5 church functions (evangelism, discipleship, fellowship, ministry, and worship), and 4 results (numerical growth, spiritual growth, ministries expansion, and mission advance). The 1-5-4 Principle is the basis for Sunday School ministry and Bible study resources.

Biblical Worldview. — As individuals experience the transforming work of God's Spirit and are confronted with the Truth of His Word, they will begin to look at life differently. They will begin to think like kingdom citizens. Because of ongoing curriculum, Sunday School has an amazing opportunity to help learners develop a biblical worldview.

Sunday School as Strategy. — Sunday School is the foundational strategy in a local church for leading people to faith in the Lord Jesus Christ and for building Great Commission Christians through Bible study groups that engage people in evangelism, discipleship, fellowship, ministry, and worship. All Bible studies assist churches and individuals in carrying out strategic Sunday School ministry.

Foundational Evangelism. — All Bible studies emphasize evangelism in every study in which the emphasis appears in the Scripture text being studied. For older children, youth, and adults, at least one session each quarter provides opportunities for lost persons to trust Christ as Savior and Lord. A plan of salvation feature appears regularly in most resources. The FAITH Sunday School Evangelism Strategy® is supported in all resources.

Foundational Discipleship.—Knowing God through Jesus is the first step of discipleship. Sunday School impacts people seven days a week, and Bible study is a foundational step for involving people in seeking the kingdom of God and fulfilling the Great Commission. Sunday School resources support all other church ministries and encourage members to strengthen their Christian walk by participating in other discipleship opportunities.

Family Responsibility.—Sunday School affirms the home as the center of biblical guidance. Bible study resources help equip Christian parents, including single parents, to fulfill their responsibility as the primary Bible teachers and disciplers of their children.

Spiritual Transformation.—A kingdom perspective of Sunday School will begin with the individual's need to experience spiritual transformation. All Bible studies compel Christians toward spiritual transformation and assist in laying foundations of the Christian faith.

Biblical Leadership.—Sunday School resources point leaders to their prophetic ministry, in which they listen to God's voice, discern His message, integrate the message into their lives, and proclaim His truth through His church to the nations. Bible study resources are built on the principle that "the leader is the lesson" in that every leader is accountable for being an authentic example of Christianity.

Teach to Transform.—All Bible studies engage learners in the biblical process of instruction that leads to spiritual transformation. Seven elements—common to all ages—guide the Bible study process: *Acknowledge Authority, Search the Truth, Discover the Truth, Personalize the Truth, Struggle with the Truth, Believe the Truth, Obey the Truth.*

The teacher has the strategic role of selecting ways to communicate the Bible message that reflect knowledge of learners, their varied approaches to learning, and their level of understanding. All Bible studies provide a well-balanced variety of interactive, age-appropriate learning activities based on eight approaches to learning:

Relational: Activities focus on interaction and cooperation with others.

Musical: Activities focus on music, singing, and performing.

Logical: Activities focus on analogies and problem-solving such as puzzles.

Natural: Activities focus on exploring elements in the natural world.

Physical: Activities focus on active involvement in projects and building skills.

Reflective: Activities focus on self-expression and personalizing Bible truths.

Visual: Activities focus on visual images and representations of what is being learned.

Verbal: Activities that focus on reading, writing, speaking, and listening.

APPROACHES TO LEARNING

Relational Barnabas	Musical David	Logical Paul
Learners Clarify Leaders can ask young adults, "What does this mean to you?"	**Learners Listen** Leaders can play a recording of the unit song and ask preschoolers to listen to what the song says.	**Learners Organize** Leaders can ask adults, "How can we address this problem? What can we do, who can do it, and when?"
Learners Affirm Leaders can encourage youth to write a note to an adult who has been a help and support to them.	**Learners Record** Leaders can provide a cassette recorder that children, youth, or adults can use for recording songs, choral readings, and so forth.	**Learners Compare/Contrast** Leaders can guide preschoolers to sort natural world items.
Learners Empathize Leaders can ask as a preschooler rocks a doll: "How do you think Miriam felt when she helped the princess with the baby Moses?"	**Learners Sing** Leaders can sing the song "You're a Special Child" to preschoolers as they arrive in the department.	**Learners Reason** Leaders can ask youth to respond to a series of *if/then* statements.
Learners Mediate Leaders can ask adults to role play a conflict and discuss how to resolve the conflict.	**Learners Compose** Leaders can ask youth to compose a song or rap that expresses the truth of the focal passage.	**Learners Analyze** Leaders can ask young adults, "Why do people act/think/live that way? What will happen to a Christian who continues to act/think/live that way?"
Learners Question Leaders can encourage youth to ask one another how they would respond to the case study.	**Learners Evaluate Music** Leaders can ask young adults to describe how the music made them feel.	**Learners Evaluate** Leaders can show a movie or video and then ask youth to identify appropriate and inappropriate responses of characters to various situations.
Learners Respond Leaders can provide props and ask older preschoolers to bring food from the homeliving area for a Food Bank.	**Learners Respond to Music** Leaders can ask adults to decide how music influences them.	**Learners Rank** Leaders can ask children to compare items, list the items in order of importance, or list things in order of their value.
Learners Discuss Leaders can guide children to discuss possible consequences of disobeying their parents.	**Learners Play Instruments** Leaders can guide children to use rhythm instruments.	**Learners Classify** Leaders can show pictures of preschoolers helping or hurting and preschoolers can tell which pictures show preschoolers helping.
Learners Dialogue Leaders can ask open-ended questions or converse with a child, asking, "What are some ways you can obey God?" or "How would you complete this sentence?"	**Learners Adapt/Create** Leaders can have youth create and sing new verses to a chorus that express things for which they are thankful.	**Learners Graph** Leaders can guide children to make a pictograph during a session, such as "God Made Me." Children indicate which boys and girls have blue eyes, brown eyes, dark hair, blond hair, and so forth.

AND TEACHING*

Natural David	Physical Ezekiel	Reflective Mary
Learners Dig/Touch Leaders can guide preschoolers to plant seeds and observe God's creative ability.	**Learners Touch** Leaders can ask young adults to join hands to form a circle to symbolize unity.	**Learners Meditate** Leaders can can encourage children to think about things they are thankful for and think about ways God is good to them.
Learners Sort/Classify Leaders can ask children to separate items into what God made and what people have made.	**Learners Recreate** Leaders can show a picture of the temple and provide blocks and props for preschoolers to build a temple.	**Learners Evaluate Themselves** Leaders can ask adults to identify one weakness in their prayer lives.
Learners Observe Leaders can ask preschoolers to observe items and processes such as the star in the center of an apple, an experiment with a magnet, a swirl in a bottle (with colored water and oil inside).	**Learners Act/Dramatize** Leaders can ask children to dress up in biblical clothes and role play the Bible story.	**Learners Contemplate** Leaders can ask young adults to consider possible results of a particular mistake in their lives.
Learners Protect Leaders can guide youth to create and implement a project that reflects Christian stewardship of creation.	**Learners Move** Leaders can ask young adults to move to the appropriate agree/disagree poster, indicating their opinions of statements the teacher makes.	**Learners Log** Leaders can have youth track the amount of time they spend this week watching television and in prayer.
Learners Reflect Leaders can help youth identify principles of science that point to an orderly Creator.	**Learners Create** Leaders can guide children to make puppets using tongue depressors, construction paper, yarn, chenille craft stems, and glue.	**Learners Write in Journals** Leaders can guide older preschoolers to draw pictures in their journals, called, "My Walk to Big Church."
Learners Collect/Display Leaders can ask members to bring examples of environmental pollution.	**Learners Manipulate** Leaders can guide preschoolers to put together a puzzle of Jesus and the children.	**Learners Study** Leaders can ask children to read a Bible verse and answer questions about it.
Learners Identify Leaders can ask members to clip photos or illustrations of items discovered in Holy Land excavations.	**Learners Play in Sports** Leaders can encourage youth to use a basketball game to exhibit Christ-likeness and open the door to witnessing.	**Learners Personalize** Leaders can ask adults to assume the role of a biblical character in a given situation and identify how the member might have responded.
Learners Plant/Cultivate Leaders can have preschoolers place seeds in a sealable plastic bag with a moist towelette.	**Learners Display** Leaders can have adults bring seemingly unrelated items to assemble/mix in class to show how parts become the whole.	**Learners Intuit** Leaders can ask youth to consider what God is directing them to do as a result of this study.

*This chart is representative, not exhaustive, of possible approaches to learning and teaching for all ages.

APPROACHES TO LEARNING AND TEACHING*

(Continued)

Visual John	Verbal Solomon
Learners Create a Mobile Leaders can ask children to illustrate one of Jesus' miracles through a mobile.	**Learners Listen** Leaders can tell adults the story of Mary and Martha.
Learners Observe Leaders can direct youth to watch a video-taped case study, following this with a discussion or written response.	**Learners Paraphrase** Leaders can ask members to rewrite and tell the parable of the lost coins into a modern-day version in story format.
Learners Diagram Leaders can ask members to sketch what they think the temple might have looked like based on the Bible's descriptions of the temple.	**Learners List** Leaders can ask children to make a list of the four Gospels or Jesus' apostles.
Learners Draw/Illustrate Leaders can provide preschoolers chunky crayons and pieces of paper for making Bible markers.	**Learners Write Ideas** Leaders can ask children to write a note to a friend or to a homebound member of the church.
Learners Demonstrate Leaders can ask children to show a project or the results of their work during the small-group time.	**Learners Use Humor/Stories** Leaders can ask youth to share humorous examples that parallel Jesus' example of the plank and the speck of dust.
Learners Propose Leaders can ask members to describe what they think Jesus might have seen when He looked out over the crowds while He hung on the cross.	**Learners Report** Leaders can instruct youth to research the meaning of key words used in a passage and report findings to the class.
Learners Paint Leaders can guide preschoolers to paint with feathers on construction paper.	**Learners Label** Leaders can open a Bible for a one-year-old and say: "This is the Bible. The Bible tells us about Jesus."
Learners Storyboard Leaders can guide youth to create a six-panel cartoon that gives the main action of the story.	**Learners Recite** Leaders can assign a psalm or other passage for groups to use in developing a dramatic monologue or responsive reading.

*This chart is representative, not exhaustive, of possible approaches to learning and teaching for all ages.

WAYS YOU CAN STUDY THIS BOOK
Self-Guided Study

Read the book, completing the personal learning activities interspersed throughout. You can do this work individually, or you might gather with a few other leaders, meeting together along the way to discuss progress. The activities provide an excellent guide for thought, application, and discussion.

All five sections in the book open with an introduction/art page; throughout each section, all personal learning activities are indicated by an art icon such as the following (for example, the adjacent art draws attention to Section 2 activities).

Group Study Plans

Meet with a group of other leaders for training in *Teaching the Jesus Way: Building a Transformational Teaching Ministry*. The 10 teaching suggestions that follow may be used in sequence to lead a group training experience of 2 1/2 hours, including break. The suggestions also may be used individually over the course of several meetings for brief training experiences. They are ideal for use each week for 10 weeks as part of a Sunday School leadership meeting. Each teaching suggestion can be accomplished in approximately 15 minutes. Although the suggestions are directed primarily toward general leaders in a church's Sunday School ministry, they are ideal for use in training with all church leaders. Teaching suggestions 1 and 2 are based on Section 1 in the book; suggestions 3 and 4, on Section 2; suggestions 5 and 6, on Section 3; suggestions 7 and 8, on Section 4; and suggestions 9 and 10 on Section 5.

1 Distribute copies of *Teaching the Jesus Way: Building a Transformational Teaching Ministry* to leaders. Use the Table of Contents (p. 3) to give a brief overview. Explain that teaching was an essential dimension of Jesus' ministry. Read aloud the title of Section 1 of the book ("He Was His Father's Son. Who Are You?"). Assign participants to one of two groups with these instructions:

> *Group 1*—Name ways Jesus' divine calling was affirmed. How did His recognition of His calling uniquely impact His teaching? Shape His mind-set?
>
> *Group 2*—Name ways you became convinced that God was calling you to your role in Sunday School. How does your recognition of your calling impact your service?

Call for the Group 1 report. Supplement responses as needed using the examples of Jesus as an adolescent in the temple and His baptism and anointing by the Holy Spirit, which affirmed Him as the Messiah. Lead a brief discussion about how Jesus' sense of calling, His relationship with the Father, and His clear purpose in life contributed to His teaching ministry. Ask: What convinced you God was calling you to a leadership role? How has that recognition impacted your service to Christ? Call for Group 2 reports. Guide leaders to complete the personal learning activity under "Has God Called You?" (pp. 28-29).

2 Explain that building a transformational teaching ministry begins with teachers who have been called by God to be a teacher, regardless of their assigned roles. Suggest that general leaders are responsible for helping a church identify, enlist, train, and equip such teachers for service. Guide leaders to review the steps for enlisting teachers (pp. 31-32).

Ask: How effective are our practices related to enlisting teachers? How might we improve our process? Guide leaders to review "My Commitment as a Sunday School Leader" (p. 33). Lead in a prayer that God would give every general leader a renewed sense of His divine calling to service and that each leader would have a deep sense of God's direction as they seek His people for service as teachers.

3 Assign leaders to work in three teams with these assignments:

Team 1: Read Matthew 4:1-11. How did the wilderness testing of Jesus reaffirm His kingdom mission?

Team 2: Read John 6:15 and 18:36. How did Jesus' encounter with the people who wanted to conscript Him as king reaffirm His kingdom mission?

Team 3: Read Matthew 16:21-23. How did Jesus' response to Peter's challenge reaffirm His kingdom mission?

Call for reports. Emphasize that Jesus had a clear sense of His mission and purpose. Ask, Do we have a clear sense of the mission and purpose for our Sunday School? Direct leaders to the definition for Sunday School (p. 12 and p. 51). Engage leaders in a brief discussion of the implications of this definition on your church's Sunday School ministry. (If time allows, ask participants to write their own definition first, comparing it to this definition.) Ask, What actions will we need to take to communicate a new way of thinking about Sunday School? Briefly overview the five Strategic Principles (pp. 52-53), guiding leaders to identify benefits of teaching in light of those principles.

4 Display a poster you have prepared with words or pictures depicting these examples of transformation: water to ice, a caterpillar to a butterfly, an egg to a chicken, and a seed to a plant. Refer to the poster and ask: What do each of these have in common? *(a type of change, or transformation)*. State that *Webster's Revised Unabridged Dictionary* defines transformed as "To change in nature, disposition, heart, character, or the like; to convert."[1] Call for a volunteer to read aloud the definition of spiritual transformation (p. 12 and p. 55). Write *Before* and *After* on two different tear sheets, and display them on a focal wall. Distribute felt-tip markers and ask leaders to list qualities of a life before and after a person experiences spiritual transformation. Guide leaders to complete the learning activity under "Has God Changed You?" (p. 61). Invite volunteers to share responses.

Deliver a minilecture on "Instruction—Three Essential Elements" (pp. 69-70). Ask leaders to identify ways they can encourage teachers to give attention to all areas. Read aloud Romans 12:2. Say: "General officers should be experiencing spiritual transformation themselves if they expect to lead teachers to teach for spiritual transformation."

5 State: "Jesus knew the message He came to communicate and taught it in a way that transformed lives." He modeled that in the encounter with a man named Nicodemus. Instruct leaders to read John 3:1-21. Guide leaders to identify statements from the Scripture passage that reflect Jesus' message of spiritual transformation.

Review the definition of spiritual transformation (p. 12 and p. 55). Ask leaders to gather in clusters of three to do some dreaming based on this question: *What would our Sunday School ministry be like if all our leaders planned and conducted their teaching in a way designed to accomplish spiritual transformation?* After a few minutes, call for responses.

Guide leaders to complete the evaluation under "Do You Know What Kind of Teaching is

Taking Place?" (pp. 87-89). Briefly discuss results. Present a brief minilecture on the "Some Guidelines for Teaching for Spiritual Transformation" (pp. 89-93). Pray that leaders will serve with a sense of spiritual power that goes beyond human limits.

6 Display three large placards on which you have written PREPARE, ENCOUNTER, and CONTINUE. (On a table nearby, place seven miniplacards on which you have written Control, Content, Concept, Context, Conflict, Conviction, and Conduct. Point out the three large placards, explaining that they represent three major teaching-learning concepts. Explain that teachers prepare not only the lesson but also themselves for the Bible teaching session and then lead pupils to encounter the God Word in a Bible study group, continuing to live and learn in daily relationships.

Use the placards and miniplacards, putting them in order as you speak, to present an illustrated minilecture on "A Plan for Teaching That Transforms" (pp. 96-102). Ask: How can we improve leadership meetings and the personal preparation done by teachers? *(Prepare)* How might giving attention to seven "C's," when teachers prepare to teach and guide learners to encounter God's Word, positively impact our church's teaching ministries? *(Encounter)* How can we more effectively help teachers continue teaching throughout the week? Learners to continue learning throughout the week? *(Continue)*

7 Display a poster on which is written "Investing in the Market." Brainstorm examples of sacrifices and benefits related to business investments; after several responses, explain that during this session leaders will explore investments in people. Briefly relate the story of Bartimaeus from Mark 10:46-52. Emphasize how Jesus looked upon the marketplace of lives with compassion and a focus on the person. State that Jesus always saw the need beneath the surface, gave His time, shared a life-changing word, and gave of Himself because He loved the person.

Ask: What ministries, actions, or disciplines would we exhibit if our Sunday School responded to others the way Jesus did? What information do we need to gather to evaluate our investment in the lives of others? Record responses. Refer to page 114.

Assert that a church's general leaders must set the pace. Guide leaders to complete the evaluation under "Leading By Example" (pp. 112-113). Call for brief comments. Pray that God will use all participants as living lessons.

8 Write the words *salt, light, water,* and *leaven* on a chalkboard. Ask, What does each word have in common? *(examples Jesus used of what we are to be and do as believers; substances that penetrate).* Ask, Is our Sunday School penetrating our community, culture, and world with the good news of Christ? Guide leaders to complete "Test the People Focus of Your Sunday School" (p. 117-119).

Lead a discussion of the results of the evaluation. Call attention to the list under "Making Intentional Plans to Invest in Others" (pp. 116-117). Discuss strategies for accomplishing items on the list. Pray that your Sunday School ministry will not be like salt that has lost its savor, but will genuinely invest itself in the lives of people.

9 State that Jesus always used teaching approaches and methodologies that were most appropriate to use for the time, setting, and people He was teaching. Distribute strips of paper, which you have labeled according to the following list. (Be sure you have at least one Scripture reference for each approach.)

Ask leaders to read aloud the Scripture passage(s) and to try to identify the teaching approach Jesus used in the passage. Refer leaders to pages 123-125 in the book.

- Luke 10:29-37; 15:11-32; Matthew 13:1-9 *(Stories)*
- Matthew 6:25-30; 18:1-4 *(Objects)*
- John 13; Luke 22:14-20, Mark 11:1-10 *(Drama)*
- John 3; John 4; Matthew 19:16-22 *(Discussion)*
- Luke 2:46; Matthew 16:13-17; Mark 10:35-40 *(Questions and Answers)*
- John 6:25-50; Matthew 5—7; John 14—17 *(Lecture)*

Ask, Does our teaching ministry provide for the planning that is necessary to be able to teach God's Word the Jesus way? Guide leaders to identify specific steps for improving annual planning, Sunday School leadership meetings, and individual preparation by teachers. Pray that your leadership team will seek to hear God and will strive to develop plans that transform lives.

10 Assign leaders to work in pairs to discuss this question: *Why is engaging learners in a balanced curriculum plan a better approach for teaching for spiritual transformation than simply allowing learners to choose topics and studies based on their immediate felt needs?* After a few minutes, call for responses. State that a balanced Bible study plan will not only address "hot topics" and "felt needs" but will also guide learners to encounters with God's Word that move them toward a mature biblical faith. Guide leaders to evaluate your church's Sunday School curriculum plan using the four points listed on pages 131-133. Review the list of characteristics of curriculum produced by LifeWay Christian Resources (pp. 129-132 and Appendix B, 150-151).

Call attention to the variety of teaching approaches (pp. 135-138 and Appendix C, pp. 152-154). Ask leaders to determine which approach reflects their preferred way to learn. Emphasize the importance of using a variety of teaching methods because of the different ways people learn.

Ask leaders to think about the transformation that has taken place in their lives from the time they first heard about Jesus until now. Ask, How are you still experiencing spiritual transformation? Pray that each will listen to God's voice through His Word; and that each leader will be able to discern God's message, integrate it into their lives, and faithfully teach it to others.

Teaching the Jesus Way: Building a Transformational Teaching Ministry Training Pack (0-6330-0841-9) contains additional help for group study of *Teaching the Jesus Way: Building a Transformational Teaching Ministry*. The pack includes one copy of the book; a video featuring Dr. Bruce H. Wilkinson; a CD-ROM with computerized presentation, visuals, and handouts for the training experience; four promotional posters; and two additional training plans (a 2 1/2-hour plan and a 5-hour plan).

[1] *Webster's' Revised Unabridged Dictionary,* "transform."

Wayne Poling is a Sunday School/FAITH ministry consultant, Sunday School Group, LifeWay Christian Resources of the Southern Baptist Convention, Nashville, Tennessee.